Exploring Ca

MW01251507

Grades 1-6

Written by S&S Learning Materials
Illustrated by S&S Learning Materials

ISBN 1-55035-778-6
Copyright 2004
Revised January 2006
All Rights Reserved * Printed in Canada

Published in the United States by:
On the Mark Press
3909 Witmer Road PMB 175
Niagara Falls, New York
14305
www.onthemarkpress.com

Published in Canada by:
S&S Learning Materials
15 Dairy Avenue
Napanee, Ontario
K7R 1M4
www.sslearning.com

© On the Mark Press • S&S Learning Materials

OTM-1056 • SSJ1-56 Exploring Canada

Canada	Gr. 1
All About Canada	2
Let's Visit Canada	3
Canadian Provinces	3-6
Wild Animals of Canada	2-3
Famous Canadians	4-8
Let's Look at Canada	4-6
Ottawa	7-9
What is Canada?	P-K
Canadian Capital Cities	4-6
Toronto	4-8
Canadian Arctic Inuit	2-3
Canadian Provinces and Territories	4-6
Canadian Government	5-8
Development of Western Canada	7-8
Canada and It's Trading Partners	6-8
Canada's Traditions and Celebrations	1-3
Fathers of Confederation	4-8
Canadian Industries	4-6
Prime Ministers of Canada	4-8
Canada's Landmarks	4-6
Elections in Canada	4-8
Amazing Facts in Canadian History	4-6
Canada's Landmarks	1-3
Citizenship and Immigration – Becoming a Canadian!	4-8
Exploring Canada	1-3
Let's Visit...	
Let's Visit Saskatchewan	2-4
Let's Visit British Columbia	2-4
Let's Visit Alberta	2-4
Let's Visit Ontario	2-4
Let's Visit Manitoba	2-4
Let's Visit Prince Edward Island	2-4
Let's Visit Nova Scotia	2-4
Let's Visit New Brunswick	2-4
Let's Visit Newfoundland and Labrador	2-4
Let's Visit Yukon Territory	2-4
Let's Visit Northwest Territory	2-4
Let's Visit Québec	2-4
Let's Visit Nunavut	2-4
Discover Canada	
Discover Québec	5-7
Discover Prince Edward Island	5-7
Discover Ontario	5-7
Discover Nova Scotia	5-7
Discover Nunavut Territory	5-7
Canadian Communities	
Farming Community	3-4
Fishing Community	3-4
Mining Community	3-4
Lumbering Community	3-4
Ranching Community	3-4
Inuit Community	3-4

 # Exploring Canada

Table of Contents

Expectations 4
Famous Canadian Tourist and Historical Attractions 5
Provincial Symbols and Other Trivia 5
Teacher Information 5
Bibliography of Canadian Resources 6
Teacher Input Suggestions 6
Reproducible Maps 10
National Anthem (English Version) 15
National Anthem (French Version) 16
Booklet A - Discovering Canada 17
Booklet B - Canada - Our Country 42
Booklet C - Let's Visit Canada 67
Student Booklet 91
Canadian History 92
Canadian Geography 119
Canada's Government 131
A Brief Look at Canada's Landmarks 151
Answer Key 169

Introduction

This book is a compilation of material for grade 1 to grade 6, to assist you in teaching your students about Canada. The primary section of this resource is divided into three sections. Each section begins with a story that will enable your students to complete the worksheets for their grade level. Topics include research, creative writing, and mathematics for primary students.

The junior section covers a wide range of topics such as the history and geography of Canada, Canadian government, and famous landmarks. The different grade levels are integrated so you will need to choose only those activities that students are comfortable with. Reproduce the necessary pages and using the booklet cover page, collate them into individual booklets for your students. This resource meets curriculum expectations including: distinguishing physical features, different levels of government, Canada's connection to the world.

 # Exploring Canada

Expectations

Students will:
1. participate in a study of the country of Canada.
2. be introduce to the concept of a map and a globe, and be shown how to use them to locate Canada.
3. be made aware that Canada is divided into ten provinces and three territories.
4. develop an awareness and recognition of the symbols that pertain to Canada.
5. develop a patriotic spirit for their own country.
6. be shown that Canada is a mosaic of different cultures.
7. become familiar with Canada's history.

Some Famous Canadian Tourist and Historical Attractions

Newfoundland & Labrador: Cape Spear National Historic Park (St. John's), Castle Hill National Park (Placentia), Gros Morne National Park (Western Seacoast), L'Anse aux Meadows National Historic Site (tip of Great Northern Peninsula), Red Bay (Southern Tip of Labrador), Signal Hill National Historic Site and Cabot Tower (St. John's Harbour)

Prince Edward Island: Green Gables House (Cavendish), Green Park Shipbuilding Museum (near Tyne Valley), Province House National Historic Site (Charlottetown), Acadian Museum of P.E.I. (Miscouche), Lucy Maud Montgomery's birthplace (New London), Micmac Indian Village (Rocky Point), Museum of Religious Art (Mont Carmel)

New Brunswick: Acadian Historical Village (Caraquet), Fort Beausejour National Historic Site (Aulac), King's Landing Historical Settlement (Fredericton), Magnetic Hill (Moncton)

Nova Scotia: Fort Anne (Annapolis Royal), Port Royal (Annapolis Basin), Bluenose II (Halifax), Halifax Citadel (Halifax), Alexander Graham Bell National Historic Park at Baddeck (Cape Breton), Marconi National Historic Site (Glace Bay)

Québec: Chateau Montebello (Montebello), The Fort Museum (Québec City), Place d'Armes (Montréal), Basilica of Sainte-Anne-de-Beaupre (Beaupre), Montmorency Falls (near Québec City)

Ontario: Old Fort Henry (Kingston), Joseph Brant Museum (Burlington), CN Tower (Toronto), Niagara Falls, Moose Factory Island (near Moosenee)

Manitoba: Mennonite Heritage Village (Steinbach), Reil House, National Historic Park (Winnipeg), St. Boniface Basilica (St. Boniface), Lower Fort Garry Historic Park (Fort Garry)

Saskatchewan: National Doukhobour Heritage Village (Veregin), Pelican Narrows (north west of Flin Flon), Batoche National Historic Park (Batoche), Fort Walsh National Historic Park (Cypress Hills)

Alberta: Head Smashed In Buffalo Jump, Hoodoos (The Badlands), Frog Lake Historic Site (Frog Lake), Royal Tyrrell Museum (Drumheller), Giant Pysanka (Vegreville), Calgary Stampede (Calgary)

British Columbia: Butchart Gardens (Victoria), Capilano Suspension Bridge(Vancouver), Barkerville Historic Park (Barkerville), Provincial Legislative Buildings (Victoria)

Yukon: S.S. Klondike (Whitehorse), Robert Service Cabin (Dawson), Jack London's Cabin and Interpretive Centre (Dawson City), Takhani Hot Springs (near Whitehorse)

Northwest Territories: Inukshuk (Stone Markers), Whitehorse, Nahanni National Park (Western Mainland), Waterfall Route along the Mackenzie Highway, Prince of Wales Northern Heritage Centre

Nunavut: Aiuyuittuq National Park Baffin Island), Northwest Passage Historic Park (Gjoa Haven), Tunooniq Theatre (Pond Inslet), Quaummaarviit Historic Park (near Iqaluit), Ellesmere Island National Park

Exploring Canada

Provincial Symbols and Other Trivia

Newfoundland & Labrador: Bird: *Atlantic Puffin*; Flower: *Pitcher Plant*; Tree: *Black Spruce*; Nickname: *The Rock*

Prince Edward Island: Bird: *Bluejay*; Flower: *Lady's Slipper*; Tree: *Red Oak*: Song: *The Island Hymn* (written by L.M. Montgomery); Nicknames: *Spud Island, Million Acre Farm, The Garden Province, Abegweit, Minegoo, The Island*

Nova Scotia: Bird: *Osprey*; Flower: *Mayflower*; Tree: *Red Spruce*; Nickname: *Land of Evangeline, Canada's Ocean Playground;* Song: *Farewell to Nova Scotia*

Québec: Bird: *Snowy Owl*; Flower: *Blue Flag*; Tree: *Yellow Birch*; Nickname: *La Belle Province*

Ontario: Bird: *Common Loon*; Flower: *White Trillium*; Tree: *White Pine*

Manitoba: Bird: *Great Grey Owl*; Flower: *Prairie Crocus*; Tree: *White Spruce*; Nickname: *Keystone Province*

Saskatchewan: Bird: *Prairie Sharp-tailed Grouse*; Flower: *Western Red Lily*; Tree: *White Birch*; Nickname: *The Wheat Province*

Alberta: Bird: *Great Horned Owl*; Flower: *Wild Rose*; Tree: *Lodgepole Pine*; Nicknames: *Princess Province, Energy Province, Sunshine Province*

British Columbia: Bird: *Steller's Jay*; Flower: *Pacific Dogwood*; Tree: *Western Red Cedar*; Nickname: *The Pacific Province*

Yukon: Bird: *Raven*; Flower: *Fireweed*; Nickname: *Land of the Midnight Sun*

Northwest Territories: Bird: *Gyrfalcon*; Flower: *Mountain Avens*; Tree: *Jack Pine*; Nickname: *Canada's Last Frontier, Land of the Polar Bear, North of Sixty*

Nunavut: Flower: *Purple Saxifrage*; Bird: *Ptarmigan*; Animal: *Canadian Inuit Dog*

Teacher Information

Canada is the second largest country in the world, and is found on the continent of North America. Canada stretches from Newfoundland & Labrador on the Atlantic coast to British Columbia on the Pacific coast, from the Arctic Ocean in the north to the 48 parallel. Canada's neighbour to the south is the United States. Canada's land mass is slightly larger than the United States, but the United States has a much larger population. In 2003, Statistics Canada estimates that there are 31 499 560 people living in Canada. Seventy-five percent live within 150 kilometres, or 100 miles, of the southern border. The northern part of Canada is uninhabited, or thinly populated because the terrain is very rugged, and the climate severe.

Canada is a diverse land. The western coastal areas are quite beautiful with towering mountains, crystal clear lakes and lush forests. The prairies are covered with fields of wheat and other grains. In the far Arctic northlands, large areas are barren or covered with snow. Canada's largest population and manufacturing centres are located near the Great Lakes and the St. Lawrence River in central Canada. Fishing villages and sandy beaches dot the Atlantic coast.

Important Facts About Our Country

Capital City - Ottawa
National Symbol - maple leaf, beaver
Official Languages - English and French
National Holidays - Canada Day, July 1
Area of Canada - 9 970 610 km2 (3 849 674 sq. mi.)

Money - Basic Unit - dollar
Population - 31 499 560 (estimated in 2003)
National Anthem - "O Canada"
Leader - Prime Minister

 # Exploring Canada

Bibliography of Canadian Resources

There are a variety of websites that you can use to explore Canada, the country or each province if you prefer. Here are some websites that can start you off.

Federal Government Websites:

Canadian Heritage	www.pch.gc.ca	Prime Minister of Canada	www.pm.gc.ca
National Library of Canada	www.nlc-blc.ca	Kids' Zone	www.pm.gc.ca/kids.asp?
Government of Canada	www.gc.ca	Canada's SchoolNet	www.schoolnet.ca

Provincial Websites:

Alberta	www.gov.ab.ca	Nunavut	www.gov.nu.ca
British Columbia	www.gov.bc.ca	Ontario	www.gov.on.ca
Manitoba	www.gov.mb.ca	Prince Edward Island	www.gov.pe.ca
Northwest Territories	www.gov.nt.ca	Québec	www.gouv.qc.ca
Nova Scotia	www.gov.ns.ca	Saskatchewan	www.gov.sk.ca
New Brunswick	www.gnb.ca	Yukon	www.gov.yk.ca
Newfoundland & Labrador	www.gov.nf.ca		

This series of individual books on each province and territory is published by S&S Learning Materials.

- SSJ1-19 - Let's Visit Prince Edward Island
- SSJ1-14 - Let's Visit Saskatchewan
- SSJ1-16 - Let's Visit Alberta
- SSJ1-15 - Let's Visit British Columbia
- SSJ1-28 - Let's Visit The Yukon
- SSJ1-30 - Let's Visit Northwest Territories

- SSJ1-18 - Let's Visit Manitoba
- SSJ1-27 - Let's Visit Newfoundland & Labrador
- SSJ1-20 - Let's Visit Nova Scotia
- SSJ1-21 - Let's Visit New Brunswick
- SSJ1-31 - Let's Visit Québec
- SSJ1-17 - Let's Visit Ontario

Teacher Input Suggestions

Planning Ahead:

Well in advance of beginning this unit in your classroom begin to collect as many of the following items as possible:

- Fiction and nonfiction books that pertain to Canada
- Photographs and pictures of famous places found in Canada
- Pictures of famous Canadians and symbols of Canada
- Crests and flags that represent the ten provinces and the three territories
- Pictures of the provincial and territorial floral emblems and birds
- A large Canadian flag
- A picture of the present Prime Minister of Canada
- Pictures of Canadian animals
- Pictures of the different types of Canadian people that make Canada a mosaic country
- Maps of Canada and the individual provinces, road maps, atlases, large floor maps, globes
- A puzzle map of Canada
- Canadian postcards
- Canadian travel brochures and pamphlets
- Samples of foods that are made in Canada
- Films, filmstrips, videos and slides that pertain to Canada
- Picture Collections: SSPC-03 - North American Animals; SSPC-10 - Inuit; SSPC-16 - Maps and Symbols of Canada; SSPC-28 - Canada; SSPC-41 - Famous Canadians
- Posters: SST1-01 - Prime Ministers of Canada; SST1-02 - Canada Map; SST1-03 - Canada's Capitals; SST1-04 - Canadian Industries; SST1-05 - Canadian Money

Exploring Canada

Bulletin Board Displays:

Use any of the suggested ideas to make a display on your bulletin board.

1. **What is Canada?** On the bulletin board place a large map of Canada. Connect string or wool to each province. At the end of each piece of string attach a card bearing the name of each province. This same display could be done on the chalkboard. Glue magnetic tape to the back of the map and to the back of provincial and territorial name cards. Use this display as part of a Mapping Centre. The children will use the name cards to place on the correct province. Have a sample map with the names of the provinces and territories on it for the students to use as a reference.

2. **Canada's Symbols**: On a bulletin board display a map of Canada. Around the map display pictures of items or three dimensional objects that represent Canada such as a small Canadian flag, a maple leaf, a beaver, the Royal Canadian Mounted Police, Canadian money, a picture of the Prime Minister and the Parliament Buildings (Ottawa), Canada's Coat of Arms, a polar bear, the Bluenose Schooner, maple syrup and totem poles. Label each symbol with a name card. Entitle the display "Symbols of Canada".

3. **Canadian Communities**: On a bulletin board display a large map of Canada. Around the map place pictures of different types of Canadian communities such as fishing, farming, mining, manufacturing, lumbering, ranching and Inuit. Connect the various communities to the areas in Canada where they are located. Entitle the display "Canadian Communities".

4. **We Are Canadians**: On a large bulletin board display a large flag of Canada. Around the flag display pictures of different families or people who are Canadians such as Caucasion, Black, Native Canadians, Inuit, Asians, Pakistanian,Sikhs, etc. Title the display "We Are Proud Canadians".

5. **Tourist Attractions**: On a bulletin board display and label famous tourist attractions. Title the display "Famous Places to Visit in Canada".

6. **Animals of Canada**: Display pictures of Canadian Animals such as the beaver, polar bear, bald eagle, snowy owl, black squirrel, grizzly bear, seal, Arctic fox, lemming, muskrat, Canada Goose, mountain sheep, moose, deer, caribou, raccoon and porcupine. Make up rhymes or riddles about each one. Print them on cards. Read the riddles or rhymes to your students or have them read them and then have them match the rhyme or riddle to each picture. Title the display "We Live in Canada Too".

7. **Famous People**: To familiarize students with famous Canadians, display pictures of these people on a bulletin board. Label each one. Discuss the importance of each famous Canadian. Title the display "We Are Famous Canadians".

8. On a chart print the words to Canada's National Anthem called "O Canada". Display the anthem on a bulletin board. Around the anthem display Canadian symbols and pictures of well known Canadian places or buildings. Use the chart to practise saying the words and singing them everyday. (See page 21 & 22)

Introductions:

Use any one of the following suggestions:

1. Play Canada's National Anthem without any words to see if the students recognize the tune. Then listen to a version that does have the vocal. Have your students sing along if they can. Play the National Anthem every day and have the students participate. It is **extremely important** that Canadian children know how to sing their own National Anthem.

2. Show a video, film or filmstrip on Canada and discuss the various places seen in the film. List their names on a chart. Put a checkmark beside any places the students have visited. This could become a graphing exercise.

 # Exploring Canada

3. Read Ted Harrison's "O Canada" to the students and discuss the pictures of the various places. Discuss the way in which the artist depicted the places and the colours he used.

4. Establish an Interest Centre entitled "Let's Look at Canada". At the centre, place Canadian souvenirs, postcards, books, dolls, foods, pictures, etc. Discuss the centre and have the students add things to it as the unit proceeds. During discussion time the students may talk about the items that they are contributing to the centre and tell where it came from in Canada. Make sure that you send a letter home to the parents of your students informing them of the topic and ask them to assist their children in locating Canadian items.

Discussion Topics:

Discuss any of the following topics with your students. Try to make a chart story after each discussion.

a) Location of Canada on a wall map and a globe

b) The concept of a village, town, city, province or territory, country

c) Size of Canada in comparison to other countries (Use a map or globe)

d) People who live in Canada - emphasize the multicultural mosaic

e) The Canadian Flag - colours, maple leaf; meaning of colours; importance of maple leaf

f) Canadian Symbols - maple leaf, Royal Canadian Mounted Police, beaver, polar bear, Bluenose Schooner, Bonhomme, Canada Goose, money

g) Landforms in Canada - rivers, lakes, waterfalls, mountains, hills, oceans, bays, islands etc. (Refer to a wall map or use pictures of the various landforms.)

h) Climate in Canada - four definite seasons: winter, spring, summer, fall; very cold in northern areas; some areas get snow while others receive a great deal of rain

i) Canadian Animals - moose, black bear, grizzly bear, polar bear, deer, beaver, raccoon, skunk, lemming, fox

j) Canadian Sports - hockey, lacrosse, baseball, basketball, track and field, swimming, etc.

k) Ottawa - Canada's Capital City; home of the Prime Minister; Parliament Buildings

l) Products grown in Canada - wheat, apples, etc.

m) The importance of Canada and why we should be proud of it

Mathematics:

Review the concept of Canadian coins and their values. Set up a store that contains Canadian two dollar coins, one dollar coins, quarters, dimes, nickels and pennies. The students can take turns being the storekeeper and the shopper. Use Canadian play money and a toy cash register. Use the activities in the unit at a Mathematics Centre. Discuss large numerals, particularly when referring to populations of provinces and cities. Review place value, sequencing numerals, collecting numerals, and reading and writing numeral words over 1 000.

Miscellaneous Ideas:

1. Plan to take your class on an excursion to a local tourist attraction.

2. Invite a local politician to your classroom to talk about the importance of Canada or the importance of your community in Canada.

3. Brainstorm with your class to see what they know about Canada before the unit and at the end of the unit. Compare the two charts.

4. Read poetry and stories pertaining to Canada. Look for folk tales and legends.

5. Encourage your students to bring in newspaper articles that their parents helped them locate about different places in Canada. Display the articles on a "Canada News" bulletin board.

6. Have a "Canada Day" or "Heritage Day" celebration in your classroom. If any of your students have an ethnic background encourage them to wear their national costume during the celebration. Perhaps they could give a little talk about their heritage. Celebrate the day with a birthday cake for Canada.

7. Plan to have a Canadian Career Day. The students could dress up as Canadian workers and talk about their jobs.

8. Establish a "Getting to Know Canada" Centre for your students. At the centre place things that you have collected that pertain to Canadian places. The items may be souvenirs, postcards, stamps, pictures, products etc. Encourage your students to add similar things.

9. Look for jigsaw puzzles that bear Canadian scenes and places. Place the puzzles at a special centre.

10. Try to locate old basal readers or anthologies that have Canadian stories. Design activities that can be used with the stories for the children to complete.

Maps:

A variety of maps are found on the following pages. These can be reproduced for the activities throughout this unit.

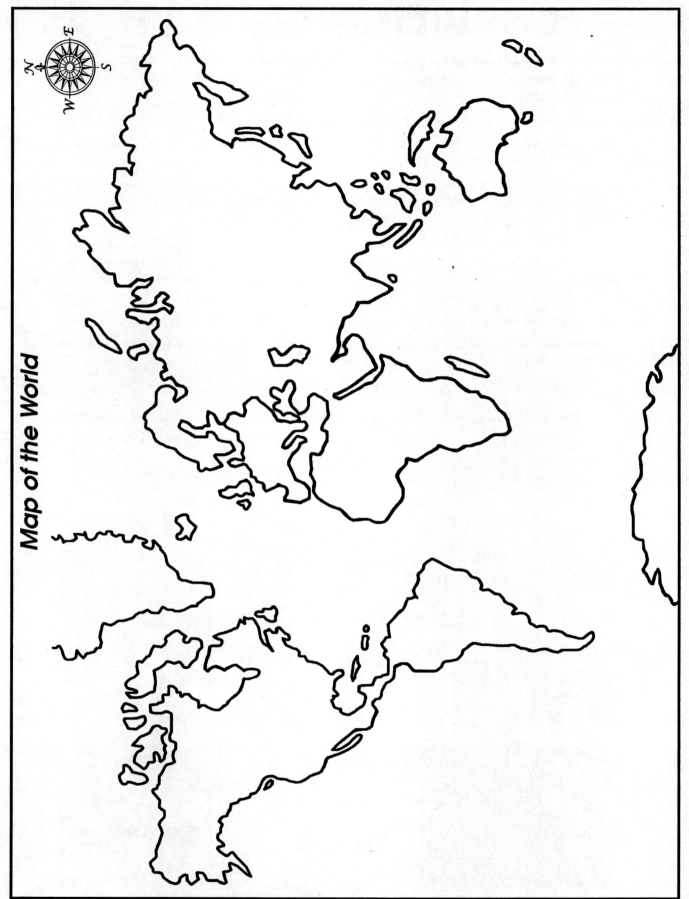

Map of the World

Name: _____

Map of the World: Where is Canada?

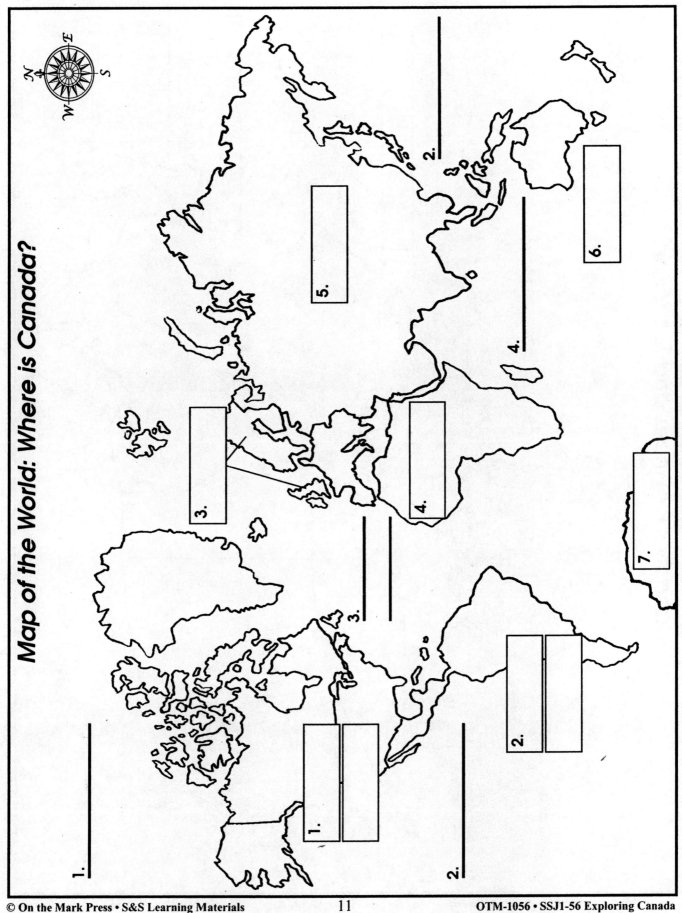

Canada's Provinces and Territories

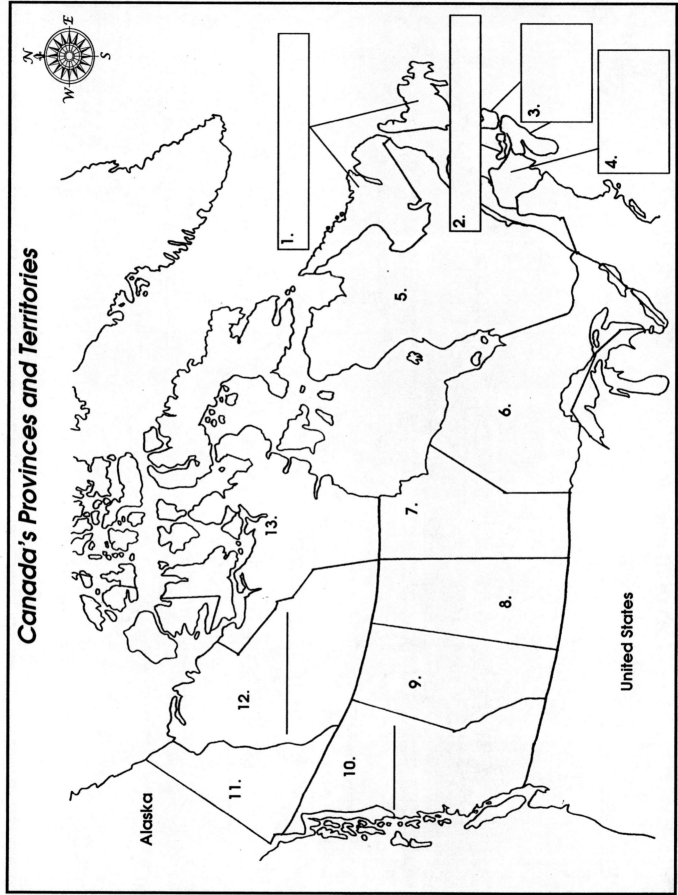

Alaska

United States

1.

2.

3.

4.

5.

6.

7.

8.

9.

10.

11.

12.

13.

Name: _____

Canada's Capital Cities

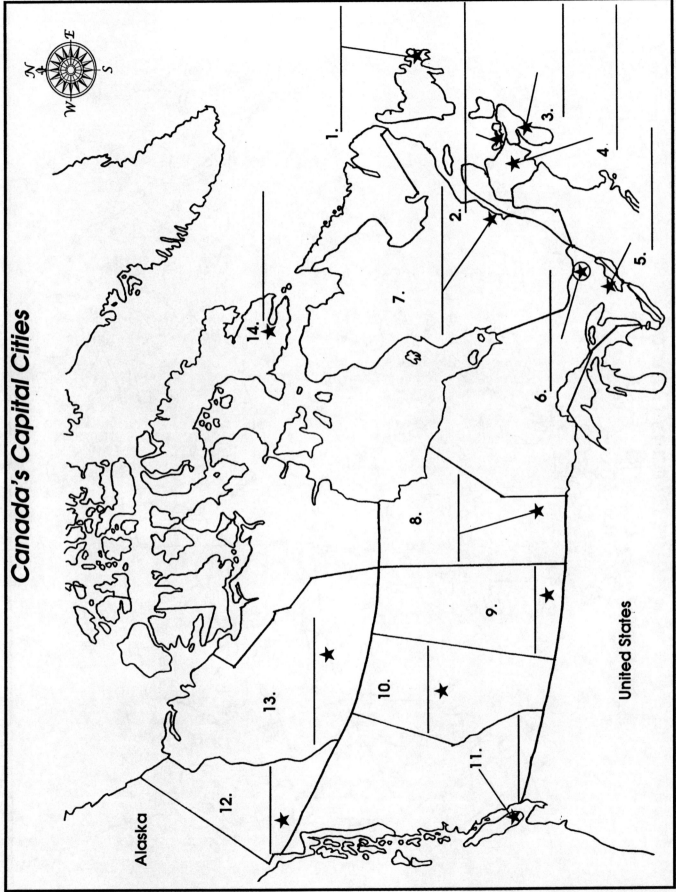

Alaska

United States

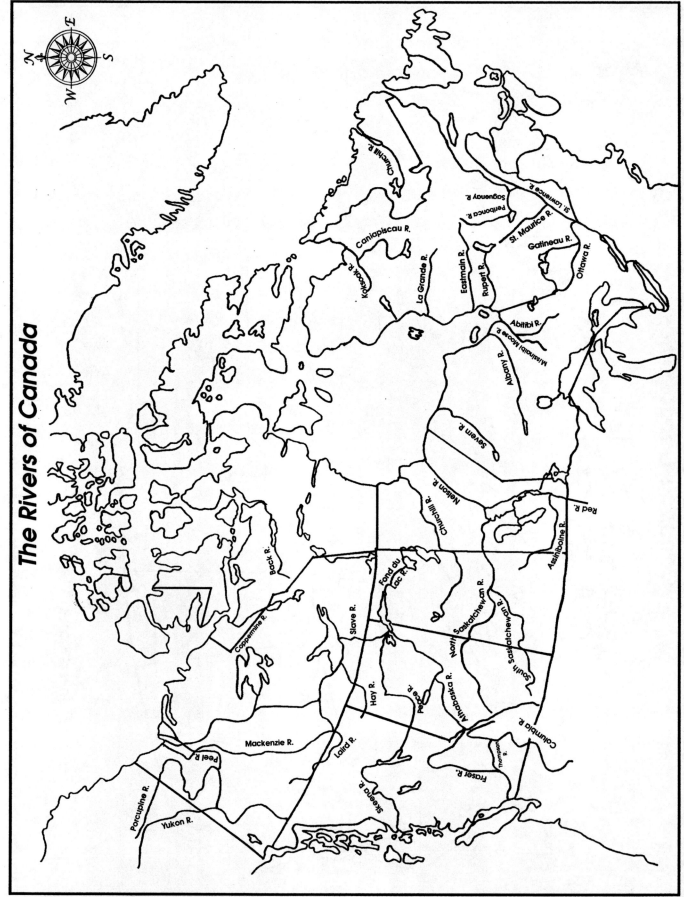

The Rivers of Canada

Churchill R.

Saguenay R.

Peribonca R.

St. Lawrence R.

Caniapiscau R.

Koksoak R.

La Grande R.

Eastmain R.

Rupert R.

St. Maurice R.

Gatineau R.

Ottawa R.

Abitibi R.

Missinaibi Moose R.

Albany R.

Severn R.

Nelson R.

Churchill R.

Red R.

Assiniboine R.

Back R.

Fond du Lac R.

North Saskatchewan R.

South Saskatchewan R.

Slave R.

Coppermine R.

Hay R.

Peace R.

Athabaska R.

Columbia R.

Mackenzie R.

Liard R.

Thompson R.

Peel R.

Fraser R.

Skeena R.

Porcupine R.

Yukon R.

Canada's National Anthem

(English Version)

O Canada

O Canada!
Our home and native land!
True patriot love in all thy sons command.

With glowing hearts we see thee rise,
The true North strong and free!

From far and wide,
O Canada, We stand on guard for thee.

God keep our land glorious and free!
O Canada, we stand on guard for thee.

O Canada, we stand on guard for thee.

Canada's National Anthem

(French Version)

<u>O Canada</u>

O Canada! Terre de nos aïeux,
Ton front est ceint de fleurons glorieux!

Car ton bras sait porter l'épée
Il sait porter la croix!

Ton historie est une épopée,
Des plus brillants exploits.

Et ta valeur, de foi trempée,
Protégera nos foyers et nos droits.

Protégera nos foyers et nos droits.

Discovering Canada

Many years ago the only people who lived in Canada were the Native People and the Inuit.
They hunted and fished for their food.

Explorers travelled by boat looking for new lands to find gold.
Jacques Cartier said Canada belonged to France.

People came from many different countries to settle in Canada.
They travelled by land and water.
They built homes of logs and sod.

Canada is a big country.

It has ten provinces.

It has three territories.

It has cities and towns.

Canada has big mountains.

Booklet A - Discovering Canada

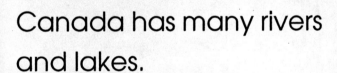

Canada has many rivers and lakes.

It has large forests.

Many wild animals live in the forests.

Booklet A - Discovering Canada
OTM-1056 • SSJ1-56 Exploring Canada

Canada has many animals.
The beaver lives in the woods.
The polar bear lives where it is very cold.
Sheep can be found in the mountains.

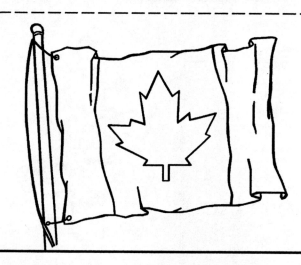

Canada has a beautiful flag.
It is red and white.
A red maple leaf is on it too.

Many people live in
Canada.
They come from
different countries.
Canadians share their
customs with each other.

People in Canada work at
many jobs.
Some people cut down trees.
Some people catch fish.
Some people work in factories.
Some people work in offices.

The capital city of Canada is called Ottawa.

The Prime Minister lives here.

The Prime Minister works at the Parliament Buildings.

✂ --

Colour your favourite character.

Booklet A - Discovering Canada

CANADA

Name: _____

Booklet A - Discovering Canada

© **On the Mark Press • S&S Learning Materials**   **OTM-1056 • SSJ1-56 Exploring Canada**

CANADA

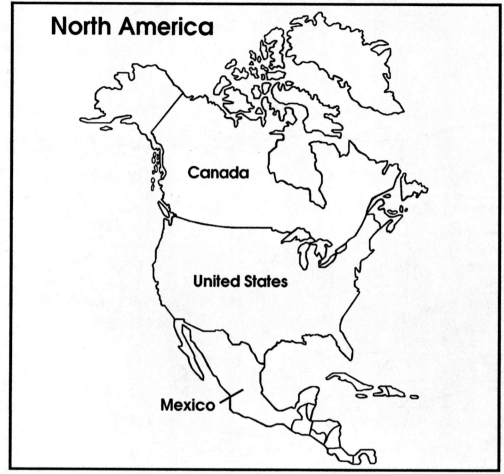

- Canada is a very _____ country.

- Its closest neighbour is the _____

  _____.

- Canada has _____ provinces.

- Canada has _____ territories.

- The capital city of Canada is called _____.

MY PROVINCE

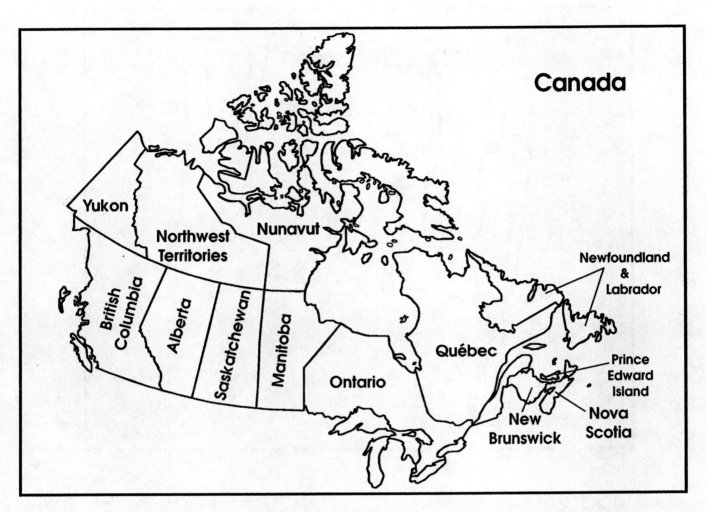

Canada

- I live in the city or town of _____.

- It is in the province of _____.

- The capital city of my province is

  _____.

- Colour the province that you live in **red**.

CANADA

- Canada has a _____ flag.

- Canadians are very _____ of it.

- It is _____ and _____.

- There is a red _____ _____ on it.

- The maple leaf has _____ points.

PEOPLE IN CANADA

- Many _____ live in Canada.

- Some of the people come from other

  _____.

- People in Canada speak different

  _____.

- Most of the people in Canada speak

  _____ or _____.

THE MAPLE LEAF

- The _____ _____ is the

  _____ of Canada.

- It is on Canada's _____ and on Canada's

  _____.

- Many _____ _____ grow
  in Canada.

- In the autumn their leaves change _____.

THE CANADA GOOSE

- The _____ _____ is a symbol of Canada.

- The Canada Goose is _____ and _____.

- The Canada Goose is a big _____.

- It flies _____ in the fall and returns in the _____.

Booklet A - Discovering Canada

OTM-1056 • SSJ1-56 Exploring Canada

THE BEAVER

- The _____ is a Canadian symbol.

- It is seen on the _____.

- It is _____ in colour.

- Its tail is _____.

- The beaver lives in a _____.

- It eats bark from _____.

Booklet A - Discovering Canada
OTM-1056 • SSJ1-56 Exploring Canada

THE ROYAL CANADIAN MOUNTED POLICE
(R.C.M.P.)

- The R.C.M.P. help look after the _____ of _____.

- An R.C.M.P. officer is a special kind of _____.

- Sometimes the R.C.M.P. officer rides a _____.

- The R.C.M.P. officer sometimes wears a red _____ and _____ pants.

- The officer's hat is _____.

© On the Mark Press • S&S Learning Materials

Booklet A - Discovering Canada

OTM-1056 • SSJ1-56 Exploring Canada

Name: _____

Brandon Beaver's Sounds

- Canada is a big country.

- **Canada** begins with the sound that "**Cc**" makes.

Print **eight** words that begin like Canada.

A) 1. _____   5. _____

   2. _____   6. _____

   3. _____   7. _____

   4. _____   8. _____

B) Say the letter **Cc**. Trace and print **C** and **c** on the lines below.

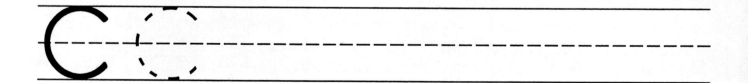

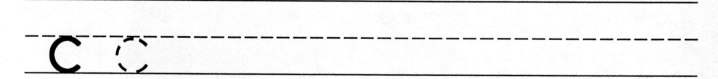

Booklet A - Discovering Canada
OTM-1056 • SSJ1-56 Exploring Canada

Brandon Beaver's Sounds

Read the word under each picture.

Print the words under the correct heading.

B Words	M Words
_____	_____
_____	_____
_____	_____
_____	_____

bee

moose

milk

beaver

mountain

bed

ball

mountie

Booklet A - Discovering Canada
OTM-1056 • SSJ1-56 Exploring Canada

Brandon Beaver's Sounds

Match the sound to the picture by drawing a line.

Example:

m

c

b

g

f

m

Brandon Beaver's Sounds

Initial Consonants and Word Endings

Cut out the sound cards and word endings.
Match them to make Canadian words.
Give the students a sheet of paper to write the answers on.

Example: 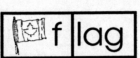 | f | lag |

	b	**olar bear**
	c	**oose**
	p	**anada**
	m	**oose**
	g	**ountie**
	m	**eaver**

Brandon Beaver's Words

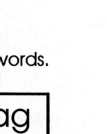

Cut out the word cards below.
Match the puzzle pieces to make Canadian words.
Can you say the words?

Example:

	Can	pole	
	totem	leaf	
	maple	ada	
	polar	ver	
	bea	tie	
	moun	bear	

Booklet A - Discovering Canada
OTM-1056 • SSJ1-56 Exploring Canada

Brandon Beaver's Tales

Many people like living in Canada.

Think of **good** things about Canada.

Finish each sentence below.

1. Canada is a good place to live because

_____

_____

_____

2. Canada is _____

_____

_____

3. I like Canada because _____

_____

_____

4. People in Canada are _____

_____

_____

Brandon Beaver's Tales

Canada has many famous places.

Have you ever visited a famous place in Canada?

Draw a picture of the famous place.

Print a story about it.

_____

_____

_____

_____

_____

Brandon Beaver's Tales

Where do you live in Canada?

Make up a story about the place where you live.

Draw a picture of the place.

My Home in Canada

I live in _____

_____

_____

_____

_____

_____

Name: _____

Brandon Beaver's Math

Colour the number of coins that match.

Print the number of the coloured coins on the line.

1. Colour the pennies orange. There are _____ pennies.

2. Colour the dimes blue. There are _____ dimes.

3. Colour the nickels yellow. There are _____ nickels.

4. Colour the quarters red. There are _____ quarters.

5. Colour the toonies brown. There are _____ toonies.

6. Colour the loonies green. There are _____ loonies.

© On the Mark Press • S&S Learning Materials

Booklet A - Discovering Canada
OTM-1056 • SSJ1-56 Exploring Canada

Brandon Beaver's Math

Match the word to the coins.

Example: 2 nickels =

1. 5 pennies

2. 10 pennies

3. 15 pennies

4. 15 pennies

5. 25 pennies

6. 5 nickels

7. 2 dimes and 1 nickel

Canada - Our Country

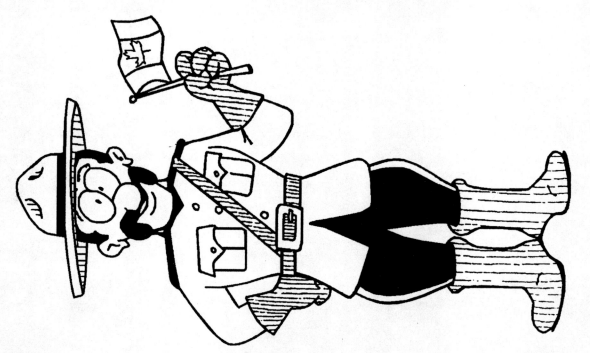

Where Is Canada?

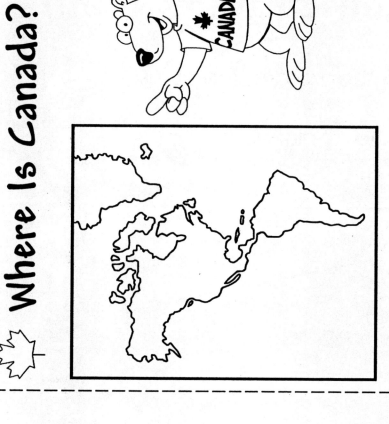

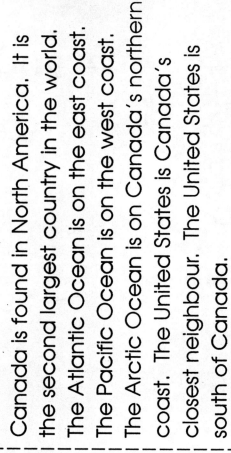

Canada is found in North America. It is the second largest country in the world. The Atlantic Ocean is on the east coast. The Pacific Ocean is on the west coast. The Arctic Ocean is on Canada's northern coast. The United States is Canada's closest neighbour. The United States is south of Canada.

Page 2   Booklet B - Canada-Our Country

Booklet B - Canada-Our Country

Canada's Capital City

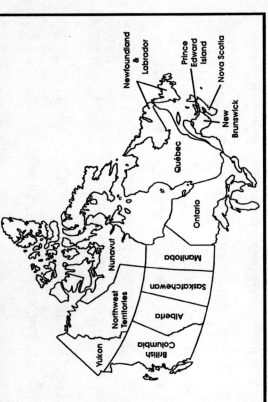

Ottawa is the capital city of Canada. It is found in the province of Ontario on the Ottawa River. The Prime Minister of Canada lives in a mansion at 24 Sussex Drive in this city. The Prime Minister is the leader of Canada. He works at the Parliament Buildings.

People like to skate on the frozen Rideau Canal in the winter. They come to Ottawa in the spring to see all the beautiful tulips.

What Makes Canada A Country?

Canada is divided into ten provinces and three territories. Each province and territory has a capital city. Québec is the largest province and Prince Edward Island is the smallest. Some of the provinces are large islands. There are many rivers and lakes in Canada.

Land Forms In Canada

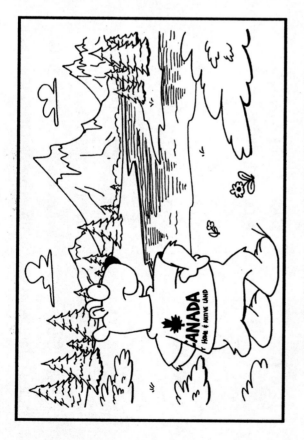

Canada has many different land forms. The Rockies are very high mountains found on the west coast. The prairies are flat, grassy lands found in the western provinces. There are many fresh water lakes and rivers in Canada. Large forests are found in every province. Many large islands can be found as well.

Who Lives In Canada?

Canada is the homeland for many different people. The Native People and Inuit have lived in Canada for thousands of years. People have come from different countries to settle and live in Canada. Most Canadian people speak English or French.

Where Do Canadians Live?

Many Canadians live in big cities. The cities are busy and filled with skyscrapers and big buildings. Some have subways for the people to travel to work.

Some Canadians live in the country. They may have farms or live in the country and work in the city.

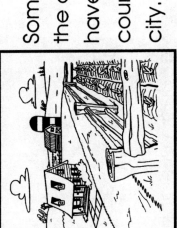

Where Do Canadians Live?

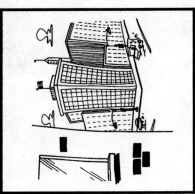

Some Canadians live in fishing communities near the Atlantic and Pacific Oceans. They fish for different types of fish, lobsters, crab, and clams. The communities are often small and very friendly.

Inuit live in the northern parts of Canada. They live in modern houses and wear present day clothes. They often travel by snowmobile, plane, and special land vehicles. Inuit follow their old ways of life and live off the land.

Where Do Canadians Work?

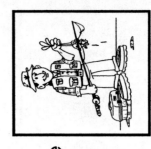

Some Canadians work in large forests. They are called lumberjacks. Their job is to cut down trees. Some people work in sawmills to make lumber or drive large logging trucks.

Some people work on farms growing food. Some farms raise beef cattle to sell.

Some Canadians make their living off the sea and they are called fishers. They get food from the sea to sell.

Where Do Canadians Work?

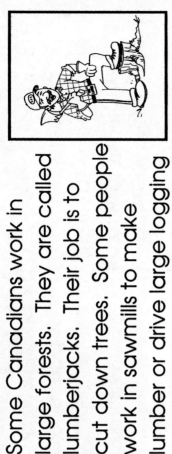

People in Canada work at many jobs.

Some people work in factories and make things.

Other people work as teachers, doctors, police officers, firefighters or store clerks and help people.

Some Canadians work in mines under the ground. They work with big drills and power tools.

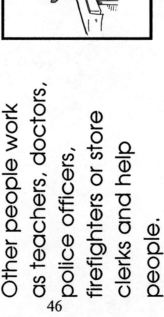

Activities in Canada

Canadians love to do many things in their free time.

In the summer they love to go swimming or boating or hiking.

Canadians enjoy watching or playing baseball, tennis or golf. During the winter Canadians go skiing, tobogganing, skating, snowshoeing, and snowmobiling or play hockey. Hockey and lacrosse are Canada's national sports.

How Do Canadians Have Fun?

In the spring, Canadians prepare their gardens and fields so they can grow things. Children like to skip, roller blade, and play marbles.

In the autumn, Canadians harvest their crops and sell them. Thanksgiving and Hallowe'en are celebrated in this season.

Many Canadians love to go to the theatres in large cities to watch famous people perform plays and musicals.

Name: _____

CANADA

_____ is the name of the largest country in North America.

It is the _____ largest country in the world.

People who live in Canada are called _____.

Canada has a population of _____.

_____ and _____ are the two main languages spoken in Canada.

Provinces and Territories of Canada

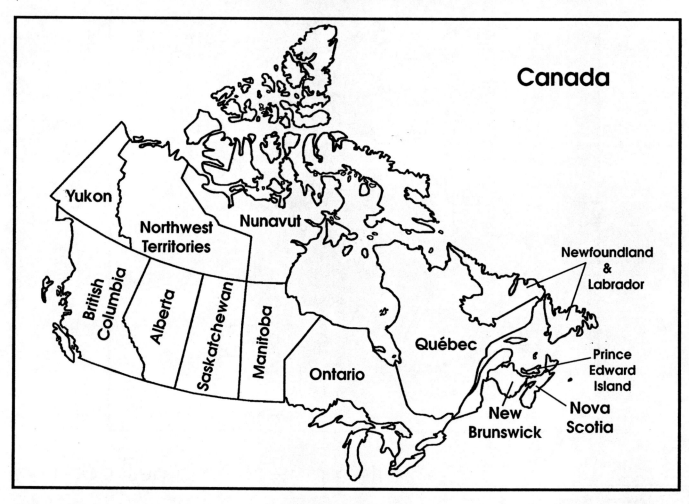

Canada is divided into ten _____ and _____ territories. Each province and territory has a _____ _____. Some of the provinces are quite _____. Newfoundland and Prince Edward Island are _____ provinces. _____ is the newest territory. It was once part of the _____ _____.

Provinces, Territories and Capital Cities of Canada

List the name of the provinces and territories. Beside each one **print** the name of its capital city.

Province	Capital City
1. _____	_____
2. _____	_____
3. _____	_____
4. _____	_____
5. _____	_____
6. _____	_____
7. _____	_____
8. _____	_____
9. _____	_____
10. _____	_____

Territory	Capital City
1. _____	_____
2. _____	_____
3. _____	_____

Name: _____

Canada's Flag

Canada's flag is _____ and

_____. It is a _____ of

Canada. In the middle of the flag is a red

_____ _____. The maple leaf

has _____ points. The maple leaf sits on

a _____ background. There are two

_____ sections on either side of the

white section. They stand for Canada's

_____.

Canada's National Symbols

The _____ _____ is a symbol of Canada.

There are many _____ trees found in Canada.

They provide Canadians with _____ and

delicious _____ _____,

The beaver was _____ and _____

for its fur for many years. It is found in many Canadian

_____.

The _____ _____ is a large bird that lives

near lakes and rivers in Canada. It flies _____ for

the winter and returns every _____.

The Royal Canadian Mounted Police (R.C.M.P.) are known

all over the _____. They wear bright _____

_____, _____ pants and brown

_____.

Canada's Capital City

_____ is the capital city of Canada.

Canada's _____ _____ are found here. The _____ protect the Parliament Buildings and the _____.

Ottawa has a _____ _____ in the spring and _____ in February.

There are many famous places in Ottawa to visit such as the Rideau _____, the _____ _____ and Rideau _____.

Canadian People

Canada is made up of a _____ of people.

Years ago people travelled by _____ to

Canada from many different _____.

The people _____ in different _____ of

Canada. Even today, people come to Canada looking

for a new _____ and a place to

_____.

Jasper P. Bear's Mathematics

Which is More?

Circle the coin or group of coins that are more.

a)	(10 cents) **or** (5 cents) (5 cents) (5 cents)
b)	(5 cents) (1 cent) (1 cent) **or** (1 cent) (1 cent) (1 cent) (1 cent) (1 cent) (1 cent)
c)	(10 cents) (10 cents) (10 cents) **or** (25 cents)
d)	(10 cents) (1 cent) **or** (5 cents) (5 cents)
e)	(25 cents) (25 cents) **or** (10 cents) (25 cents)
f)	(10 cents) (10 cents) (25 cents) **or** (10 cents) (10 cents) (10 cents) (10 cents)
g)	(5 cents) (1 cent) (10 cents) **or** (10 cents) (25 cents) (5 cents)
h)	(5 cents) (5 cents) (5 cents) **or** (10 cents) (1 cent) (1 cent) (1 cent)

Jasper P. Bear's Mathematics

How Much Altogether?

a) 5 cents + 4 cents = _____ cents

b) 6 cents + 3 cents = _____ cents

c) 2 cents + 8 cents = _____ cents

d) 3 cents + 3 cents = _____ cents

e) 9 cents + 6 cents = _____ cents

f) 8 cents + 5 cents = _____ cents

g) 7 cents + 8 cents = _____ cents

h) 9 cents + 5 cents = _____ cents

i) 10 cents + 7 cents = _____ cents

Jasper P. Bear's Mathematics

How Much is Left?

a) 15 cents - 9 cents = _____ cents

b) 12 cents - 8 cents = _____ cents

c) 13 cents - 5 cents = _____ cents

d) 11 cents - 9 cents = _____ cents

e) 15 cents - 5 cents = _____ cents

f) 11 cents - 5 cents = _____ cents

g) 13 cents - 6 cents = _____ cents

h) 14 cents - 7 cents = _____ cents

i) 16 cents - 8 cents = _____ cents

Jasper P. Bear's Mathematics

Can You Solve the Problems?

1. Mary had 10 pennies to spend. She bought some gum for 5 cents. How much did she have left?

   _____

2. Andrea had 10 cents in her piggy bank. She added 3 pennies. How much is in her bank now?

   _____

3. Peter had 5 cents, Billy had 3 cents an Paul had 6 cents. How much money did the boys have all together?

   _____

4. Tom had 15 cents to spend. He bought a balloon for 5 cents. How much money does he have left?

   _____

5. Susan went to the store with 12 cents. She bought some candy for 8 cents. How much money does she have left?

   _____

6. Mary's grandfather gave her 3 nickels. How much money does she have?

   _____

Jasper P. Bear's Thinking

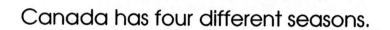

Canada has four different seasons.

They are summer, winter, spring, and autumn.

In which season do we see the following things in Canada?

1. People skiing in the mountains. _____

2. Children swimming in a pool outside. _____

3. The leaves on the trees turning yellow, red, and orange. _____

4. The grass turning green. _____

5. People raking up the leaves. _____

6. Daffodils and tulips blooming in gardens. _____

7. Children making a snowman. _____

8. People dressed in shorts and t-shirts. _____

9. People waterskiing on a lake. _____

10. Children sliding down a hill on a toboggan. _____

Jasper P. Bear's Words

Jasper has a Word Puzzle for you to solve.

Read his clues carefully.

1.
2.
3.
4.
5.
6.
7.
8.
9.
10.

province
maple leaf
beaver
hockey
territory
flag
country
mountains
ten
Ottawa

1. It is on our flag.
2. Québec is a _____.
3. A Canadian animal
4. The Yukon is a _____.
5. Canada's capital city

6. A favourite Canadian sport
7. It is red and white.
8. The number of provinces
9. Canada is a big _____.
10. Very high hills

Jasper P. Bear's Sounds

The "**skunk**" is a smelly Canadian animal.

The word "**skunk**" ends with the sound that "**k**" makes.

Copy and **complete** each word with the correct last sound.

Use the letters in the box.

t r m d x f k l r g n s

1. wol _____

2. el _____

3. ow _____

4. bea _____

5. raccoo _____

6. walru _____

7. fla _____

8. opossu _____

9. islan _____

10. rabbi _____

11. fo _____

12. dolla _____

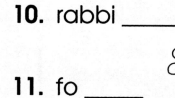

Jasper P. Bear's Sounds

Vowel sounds are heard in many Canadian words.

Print the words found in the box in the correct flag.

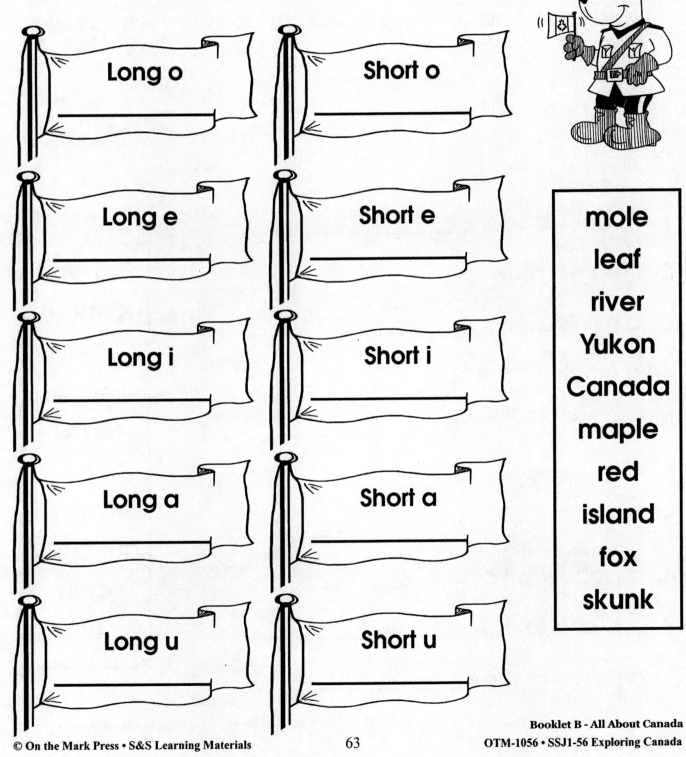

Long o	Short o
Long e	Short e
Long i	Short i
Long a	Short a
Long u	Short u

mole
leaf
river
Yukon
Canada
maple
red
island
fox
skunk

Jasper P. Bear's Sounds

The "**chipmunk**" lives in many Canadian forests.

The word "**chipmunk**" begins with the "**ch**" sound.

Can you **think** of other words that begin with "**ch**"?

The clues below will help you.

Use the words in the box for the answers.

1. to cut wood _____

2. fried potatoes _____

3. a bird's sound _____

4. a clock does this _____

5. smoke goes up it _____

6. a small boy or girl _____

7. part of your face _____

8. a baby farm bird _____

9. a place to sit _____

10. a place to pray _____

chop
church
chime
chirp
child
chair
chick
chimney
chin
chips

Jasper P. Bear's Research

There are many animals living in Canada.

Choose **one** of the animals below.

beaver	**raccoon**	**rabbit**	**fox**
moose	**polar bear**	**squirrel**	**wolf**
muskrat	**musk ox**	**chipmunk**	**deer**

Find out **three** interesting facts about the animal.

Illustrate the animal too.

Example:

The Skunk	
_____ _____ _____ _____ _____ _____ _____	

Jasper P. Bear's Research

Mapping Fun!

Look at a map of Canada. Locate **ten** different places you would like to visit. Choose **one** that is of special interest.

Find out **three** interesting facts about it.

Write a story, using complete sentences to tell about this special place and why you would like to visit.

Booklet B

Jasper P. Bear's Research

Creative Writing

There are many books written about Canada.

Make your own **book** about Canada.

In your book, **draw** pictures of things that you see in Canada.

Print a sentence or two about each picture.

Booklet B - All About Canada

Canada

Canada is a big _____ found in _____. The word "Canada" comes from a native word that means _____.

Canada is the _____ largest country in the world. Its closest neighbour is the _____.

The _____ is found on the East Coast. The _____ is found on the West Coast. The _____ is found on the Northern Coast.

Let's Visit Canada

Name: _____

Parts of Canada

Canada is divided into _____ provinces and _____ territories.

Each province and territory has a capital city.

On the chart below list the provinces, territories, and their capital cities.

Provinces

Name of Province	Capital City
1.	
2.	
3.	
4.	
5.	
6.	
7.	
8.	
9.	
10.	

Territories

Name of Territory	Capital City
1.	
2.	
3.	

Canada

Canada is divided into ten _____ and three _____. Most of Canada's _____ people live in _____. Nunavut.

The capital city of Canada is _____. It is located in the province of _____. The Prime Minister of Canada is _____. He/She is the leader of _____.

Canada's _____.

Canada's national anthem is called _____. Canada's national motto is "A Mari Usque ad Mari" which means _____.

Colour each province and territory a different colour. Colour the oceans blue.

Provinces and Territories

The Western provinces are _____ and _____. In Manitoba and Saskatchewan there are very large _____ and farmers grow _____. In Alberta there are many _____. British Columbia is filled with many large _____ that are cut down for _____.

(maps: British Columbia, Alberta, Saskatchewan, Manitoba)

The Atlantic Provinces are found on the _____ coast of Canada. They are _____, _____, _____ and _____. The _____ province in Canada is Prince Edward Island. _____ is an important industry in these provinces. Many tourists visit the Atlantic Provinces every year to see all the beautiful scenery and historical places.

(maps: Nova Scotia, P.E.I., New Brunswick, Newfoundland and Labrador)

Provinces and Territories

Canada is divided into _____ and _____. The _____ largest province is _____. The people in Québec speak mainly _____. Québec has two large cities - _____ and _____. The main industry in Québec is _____.

(map: Québec)

_____ is Canada's second largest province in size. More than _____ of the people living in Canada live in Ontario. _____ and _____ are the two main cities. Ottawa is the capital city of all of Canada. Toronto is the capital city of Ontario. Ontario's main industry is making _____.

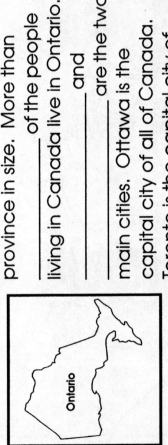

(map: Ontario)

Canada

Provinces and Territories

Nunavut

Northwest Territories

Yukon

The Canadian North is made of _____ territories.

They are the _____, _____ and _____. Nunavut is

the _____ territory where many of Canada's _____ people live. The _____ live mainly in the Northwest Territories. Canada's northland is _____. The main industries here are _____ and _____ and _____. The people depend on large boats and planes to bring in their supplies. Travelling from place to place is done by special land vehicles. Airplanes, boats, snowmobiles, and dog sleds are still used.

Canada's Capital City

Ottawa

Ottawa is the _____ city of Canada. It is found in the province of _____ on the _____.

The _____ are located on Parliament Hill in Ottawa. Many people who live in Ottawa work for the _____. The _____ and other _____ live and work in Ottawa too. They make _____ and plans for the country.

In Ottawa there is a famous canal called the _____. In the winter, people like to _____ on it during _____. In the spring, tourists come to Ottawa for the _____. At that time of the year Ottawa is quite colourful.

The Canadian Flag

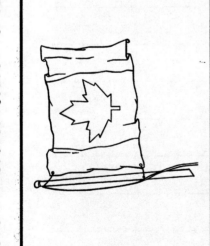

The Canadian Flag is a _____ emblem. It is _____ and _____ in colour. In the centre of the flag on a white background is a red _____. The _____ maple leaf has _____ points. The red colour stands for _____ and the white colour stands for _____. Canada's flag became our official flag on _____. Canada's _____ earlier flag was the _____, which is the flag that represents England.

Name: _____

Maxine Maple Leaf's Sounds

Discovering Vowels

Vowels are letters found in most Canadian words.

Vowels can make **two** sounds but sometimes they are **silent**.

Copy the words below neatly.

Circle each vowel sound that you can **hear** and put a **line** through the ones that are **silent**.

Beside each word, **name** the ones that you hear.

Example: | b (e) á v é r   long e |

1. polar bear _____
2. porcupine _____
3. chipmunk _____
4. province _____
5. maple syrup _____
6. totem pole _____
7. Manitoba _____
8. Nunavut _____
9. village _____
10. Whitehorse _____

Loui Lumberjack's Word Study

Make it Mean More Than One!

A village is a small place where people live.

There are many villages in Canada.

The word **village** is a **singular** word.

The word **villages** is a **plural** word.

Copy the words below neatly.

Beside each word, write its **plural form**.

1. maple leaf _____
2. territory _____
3. province _____
4. city _____
5. moose _____
6. community _____
7. deer _____
8. Canada Goose _____
9. Arctic Fox _____
10. country _____
11. ocean _____
12. walrus _____

Loui Lumberjack's Word Study

Canada's Crossword Puzzle

Think Canada!

Complete the crossword puzzle.

Read the clues carefully.

Across:

1. Canada's national emblem
2. The Yukon is one of them
3. Canada's national bird
4. It is Canada's newest territory.
5. Grain that is grown on the Prairies
6. One of the colours found on Canada's flag

Down:

1. The Rockies are high ones.
3. Canada is the second largest one.
7. The short way to write "mountie"
8. It is a red and white Canadian symbol.
9. The capital city of Canada
10. Canada has ten of them.
11. Canada's national animal
12. The name of Canada's national anthem

Fiona Fisher's Map Reading

Canadian Cities

Canada has many large cities.

A city is a large place where many people live.

Look at a map of Canada.

Find the names of **ten** cities.

Write their names in a list.

Example:

Canadian Cities

1. Ottawa
2. _____
3. _____
4. _____
5. _____
6. _____
7. _____
8. _____
9. _____
10. _____

Fiona Fisher's Map Reading

Canadian Bays

A bay is a part of an ocean, sea, or lake extending into the land.

Look at a map of Canada.

Locate **six** bays.

Write their names in a list.

Example:

Canadian Bays

1. Hudson Bay

2. _____

3. _____

4. _____

5. _____

6. _____

Cochrane Cowboy's Report

A Famous Canadian Place

Canada is filled with many interesting places to visit.

Example:

Casa Loma, Toronto

Choose a **famous** place in Canada. **Research** the one that you chose. **Complete** the worksheet on the place that you chose.

A Famous Canadian Place

Name of Place: _____

Location: _____

_____

Interesting Facts: (Try to find five.)

_____

_____

_____

_____

_____

Illustrate the famous place.

Name: _____

Cochrane Cowboy's Report

Who Lives in a Canadian Forest?

In Canada's forests many wild animals make their homes.

Example:

Choose a **Canadian** animal that interests you. **Research** the animal that you chose. **Complete** the worksheet on the animal that you chose.

A Canadian Animal

Name: _____

Appearance: (Describe how it looks.)

_____

_____

_____

Home: (Describe its home.)

_____

_____

_____

Food: (List the things that it eats.)

_____

_____

_____

Enemies: (Tell who it fears.)

_____

_____

Habits: (Tell about things it always does.)

_____

_____

On another sheet of paper illustrate the animal.

Cochrane Cowboy's Report

Writing About a Province or Territory

In Canada there are ten provinces and three territories. **Choose** a province or a territory that you find interesting. **Research it. Complete** the worksheet on the one that you chose. **Write** the information in complete sentences.

A Canadian Province or Territory

Province/Territory: _____

Capital City: _____

Size and Location: _____

_____

_____

_____

Population: _____

Products: _____

_____

_____

Interesting Facts: (Try to find six.)

_____

_____

_____

_____

_____

_____

_____

Illustrate the provincial or territorial flower and flag on another sheet of paper.

Iona Inuit's Mathematics

Place Value Fun!

A) What is the place value of each number?

Numeral	Thousands	Hundreds	Tens	Ones
1. 5632	_____	_____	_____	_____
2. 733	_____	_____	_____	_____
3. 2 063	_____	_____	_____	_____
4. 9 980	_____	_____	_____	_____
5. 607	_____	_____	_____	_____
6. 1 851	_____	_____	_____	_____
7. 3 954	_____	_____	_____	_____
8. 273	_____	_____	_____	_____

B) What is the place value of each circled numeral?

1. 5 ⑥ 2 7 _____

2. 9 0 7 ① _____

3. ⑧ 7 4 3 _____

4. 2 6 ⑨ 5 _____

Iona Inuit's Mathematics

Expanding Numerals

A) Write the numerals below the long way.

Example: $3\,653 = 3\,000 + 600 + 50 + 3$

1. $5\,905 =$ _____ + _____ + _____ + _____
2. $9\,786 =$ _____ + _____ + _____ + _____
3. $653 =$ _____ + _____ + _____ + _____
4. $8\,002 =$ _____ + _____ + _____ + _____
5. $7\,504 =$ _____ + _____ + _____ + _____
6. $2\,065 =$ _____ + _____ + _____ + _____
7. $1\,111 =$ _____ + _____ + _____ + _____
8. $6\,731 =$ _____ + _____ + _____ + _____
9. $956 =$ _____ + _____ + _____ + _____
10. $3\,605 =$ _____ + _____ + _____ + _____

B) Write the numeral that comes next.

1. $5\,631,$ _____
2. $760,$ _____
3. $8\,069,$ _____
4. $7\,213,$ _____
5. $5\,000,$ _____
6. $4\,999,$ _____
7. $6\,339,$ _____
8. $889,$ _____

Booklet C - Let's Visit Canada
OTM-1056 • SSJ1-56 Exploring Canada

Iona Inuit's Mathematics

Writing Numerals the Short Way

A) Collect the numerals to write one big numeral.

1. 1 000 + 500 + 60 + 1 = _____

2. 2 000 + 70 + 5 = _____

3. 600 + 60 + 6 = _____

4. 9 000 + 900 + 90 + 9 = _____

5. 5 000 + 1 = _____

6. 3 000 + 60 + 3 = _____

7. 800 + 90 + 6 = _____

8. 7 000 + 900 + 50 + 3 = _____

B) Count by 1's. Fill in the missing numerals.

1. 4 563, _____, _____, _____, _____

2. 2 019, _____, _____, _____, _____

3. 3 459, _____, _____, _____, _____

4. 681, _____, _____, _____, _____

5. 1 001, _____, _____, _____, _____

6. 6 781, _____, _____, _____, _____

Name: _____

Iona Inuit's Mathematics

Reading and Writing Numerals

A) Collect the numerals to write one big numeral.

1. five hundred forty-one _____
2. one thousand fifty-one _____
3. eight hundred seventy-three _____
4. five hundred thirteen _____
5. six thousand one hundred and two _____
6. eleven hundred and two _____
7. four thousand nine hundred six _____
8. one thousand five hundred eleven _____
9. three thousand two hundred _____
10. nine thousand seven hundred forty _____

B) Print the numeral that comes before and after.

1. _____ , 9 631, _____   5. _____ , 8 019, _____
2. _____ , 3 260, _____   6. _____ , 6 000, _____
3. _____ , 2 003, _____   7. _____ , 710, _____
4. _____ , 699, _____   8. _____ , 7 613, _____

Iona Inuit's Mathematics

Writing Numerals as Number Words

A) Write each numeral below as a numeral word.

1. 505 - _____

2. 1 673 - _____
   _____

3. 5 640 - _____
   _____

4. 2 531 - _____
   _____

5. 3 030 - _____
   _____

6. 4 871 - _____
   _____

7. 699 - _____
   _____

8. 9 380 - _____
   _____

B) Is the first numeral **greater** than (>) or **less** than (<) the second numeral?

1. 5 633 _____ 1 642
2. 660 _____ 6 660
3. 540 _____ 249
4. 1 112 _____ 112
5. 1 231 _____ 1 321

6. 7 031 _____ 8 431
7. 1 602 _____ 6 102
8. 7 654 _____ 7 649
9. 2 131 _____ 2 013
10. 996 _____ 9 966

Constable MacKenzie's Reading

Have You Ever Seen?

Complete each rhyme with the correct pair of rhyming words.

1. Have you ever seen a polar _____ ,
   Eating a prickly _____ ?

2. Have you ever seen a silly _____ ,
   Trying to eat crayfish with a _____ ?

3. Have you ever seen a Canadian _____ ,
   Chop down a tree with a sharp _____ ?

4. Have you ever seen a musk _____ ,
   Wearing woolly pink _____ ?

5. Have you ever seen a mountain _____ ,
   Floating on a river in a row _____ ?

6. Have you ever seen a stinky _____ ,
   Make his home in an old _____ ?

7. Have you ever seen a _____ ,
   Travelling with a Canada _____ ?

8. Have you ever seen a _____ ,
   Driving a big logging _____ ?

woodchuck	**socks**	**boat**	**skunk**	**truck**
moose	**bear**	**spoon**	**ox**	**goat**
trunk	**goose**	**beaver**	**pear**	**raccoon**
cleaver				

Constable MacKenzie's Reading

Riddle Fun!

Read each riddle carefully.

Print the name of the province on the line provided.

1. This is a western province. It is the province between Saskatchewan and British Columbia. The capital city is Edmonton.

   The province is _____ .

2. This is not a province. It lies between two other territories. Yellowknife is the capital city.

   The place is _____ .

3. It is a western province. It is found between Manitoba and Alberta. Wheat is grown in this province.

   It is called _____ .

4. This province is found on the west coast of Canada. Victoria is its capital city. Delicious apples and salmon are found here.

   It is the province called _____ .

5. It is Canada's largest province. Many people speak French here. Its capital city has the same name. Maple syrup comes from this province.

   It is called _____ .

6. It is an island and the smallest province in Canada. Potatoes grow well in its red dirt. Charlottetown is its capital city.

   It is called _____ .

Constable Mackenzie's Reading

7. It is found between Manitoba and Québec. Its capital city is Toronto. Most of the people in Canada live here.

   It is called _____ .

8. It is a province made of two parts. Part of it is an island. Its capital city is called St. John's.

   It is called _____ .

9. It is the closest prairie province to Ontario. Buffalo used to roam over its land. Winnipeg is the capital city.

   It is called _____ .

10. It is an Atlantic province. It is a small province. Cape Breton Island is part of it. Its capital city is Halifax.

    It is called _____ .

11. Its capital city is Fredericton. It is found between Québec and Nova Scotia. There are many forests here. It is one of the Atlantic provinces.

    It is called _____ .

12. It is the smallest territory. It became famous when gold was found here. Whitehorse is its capital city.

    It is called _____ .

13. It is Canada's newest territory. Many Inuit people live here. Its capital city is Iqaluit.

    It is called _____ .

Farmer Fraser's Creative Writing

A Canadian Postcard

A postcard has a picture of a place on one side and a space to write a note and an address on the back.

When we visit another country or another province we often send postcards to our friends and relatives.

Example:

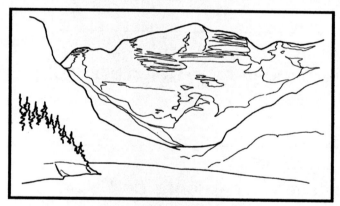

Front

Rocky Mountains

Dear David,
Having a great trip!
The Rockies are
beautiful.

Love Mary

David Taylor
609 Apple Cres.
Winnipeg, MB.
Canada
R1H 7B3

Back

Choose a place that tourists like to visit.

Design a postcard for the place.

On your postcard **illustrate** a famous place.

Booklet C - Let's Visit Canada
OTM-1056 • SSJ1-56 Exploring Canada

Farmer Fraser's Creative Writing

Write a Canadian Poem

Each province in Canada has special features and places.

Print the name of your province vertically.

Example:

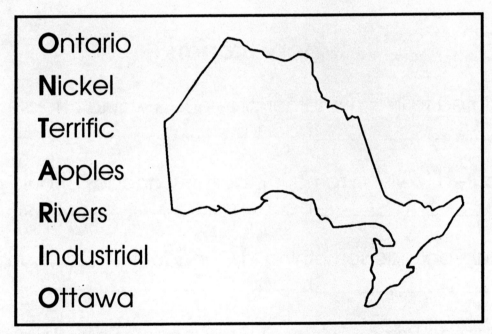

Ontario
Nickel
Terrific
Apples
Rivers
Industrial
Ottawa

Think of words that describe your province or the things that it contains.

Each word must **begin** with a letter in your province's name.

Illustrate your one word poem.

Farmer Fraser's Creative Writing

Write a Story

Choose **one** of the story starters below.

Copy the story starter neatly.

Complete it.

Add more sentences to it and write a story.

Story Starters

1. If I wanted to live in another province, I would choose _____because ....

2. If I wanted to visit a famous place in Canada, I would choose _____because ....

3. If I could change something in Canada, I would change _____because ....

4. If I could be Prime Minister of Canada for a day, I would be _____because ....

5. If I could be a famous Canadian, I would want to be _____because ....

Exploring Canada

Name: _____

 # Exploring Canada

An Introduction to Canada

Canada is a very large country with a variety of climates, vegetation and landforms. Within its border you can find tall mountains, vast plains, thousands of lakes and large stretches of forest. Canada will let you experience hot summers and icy winters. There are large metropolitan centres where people from all over the world come to work or play. There are small villages that make the visitor feel like they have stepped back in time to a setting in the 1800s. Canada is definitely a land of contrasts.

It is easy to find Canada on a map of the world because it is so big in size. You can see why the Canadian motto is "From Sea to Sea" when you realize just how big this country is. It is the second largest country (in land mass) in the world. Located in the continent of North America, Canada lies on the northern border of the United States, with the Atlantic Ocean to the east, the Pacific Ocean to the west and the Arctic Ocean to the north. This country stretches just over 5 000 kilometres from east to west.

Because of its size and climatic conditions, exploration of Canada took a long time. Canada is a young country, when you compare it to the countries in Europe. It was settlers from Europe who helped to establish farms and villages throughout Canada and gradually helped it to grow from a small colony to an independent nation.

Though Canada has only been a nation since 1867, it is recognized as a leader in medical and technological research as well as the supplier of much of the world's resources. Canada's population may be less than that of countries with a much smaller area, but her contribution to the world community is formidable.

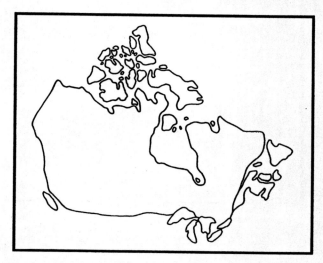

 # Exploring Canada

Name: _____

An Introduction to Canada

Read the Information Card entitled "An Introduction to Canada".

Complete the following activities.

1. Why would visitors to Canada feel they had many choices in the types of activities they might want to experience?

   _____

   _____

   _____

   _____

   _____

2. Using a geography resource book, find the ten largest countries in land mass, and list them from the largest to the smallest. Underline Canada in red.

   _____

   _____

   _____

   _____

   _____

   _____

   _____

   _____

3. What problems would explorers have had in trying to cross the country of Canada?

   _____

   _____

   _____

   _____

4. Using the library or internet as a resource, make a list of five to eight books or websites that would help you find out more about Canada. On a separate sheet of paper, record the information for each. Be prepared to present your findings to the class.

Exploring Canada

The First Canadians

There have been many theories as to who the first Canadians were or when they came to Canada. However, most scientists and historians seem to agree that the first people to arrive in Canada came by way of a "land bridge" that at one time connected Northern Russia and Alaska.

The people that we know as Native Canadians and Inuit are the descendants of these first immigrants to North America. Scientists believe that the first people to enter Canada did so about 30 000 years ago. They were tribes of ancient hunters, following the animals they killed for their food. At that time, before the end of the last Ice Age, these people were able to cross from the area where they lived, Northern Russia, and gradually moved into northern Canada. Over a period of thousands of years, their descendants gradually moved south, still following the animals that they depended upon for food and clothing.

Some of these people eventually reached South America. Many settled down in various parts of Canada and the United States to become the Native Canadians and Inuit that we are familiar with today.

The "land bridge" no longer exists. After the last Ice Age, the increase in the level of the ocean water caused the bridge to disappear beneath what we know as the Bering Strait. The ancient hunters were now "trapped" in the New World and it would be more than 10 000 years before new explorers set foot in Canada.

 # Exploring Canada

Name: _____

The First Canadians

Read the Information Card entitled "The First Canadians".

Complete the following activities.

1. Obtain a map of the world from your teacher. Locate Canada on the map. Show the route that the early Natives took as they moved from Asia to North America.

2. Who are the Inuit? What does the word mean? Where do they live today?

   _____
   _____
   _____
   _____
   _____
   _____

3. Why did it take so long for North America to become settled by the Natives?

   _____
   _____
   _____
   _____

4. Why do you think some hunters chose to stay in the Arctic regions of North America while others moved south and settled in warmer areas?

   _____
   _____
   _____
   _____

5. When did the land bridge disappear and why did this happen?

   _____
   _____
   _____
   _____
   _____

Exploring Canada

Vikings - Warriors and Explorers

The first Europeans to set foot in Canada were the Vikings. They came from that area in Europe called Scandinavia - the countries of Denmark, Norway and Sweden. These brave people were used to violent storms, rough seas and many weeks of travel on the ocean.

The Vikings had already settled on two northern islands, Iceland and Greenland. They had decided to explore further west hoping to find a place of rich farmlands and other treasures. Historians believe that the Vikings probably landed in North America about the year 1 000 A.D. Their first landing site was most likely Baffin Island. They were not impressed with the barren coast of flat stones and cold weather.

The Vikings were adventurous enough to continue their search for new land from "Helluland", the name they gave to Baffin Island to the area we know today as the Labrador coast, which they named "Markland".

They were still not truly satisfied with the results of their journeys and pressed on towards the south. In an area known today as Cape Cod, which they called "Vinland", they finally found the fertile farmland they had been seeking. The climate was good, their cattle would be able to stay outside all year and grapes grew in great numbers. However, there was one problem, The Vikings and the Native inhabitants of the area did not get along at all. The Viking colony only lasted a few years before the "Skraelings", their name for the Natives of that area, forced them to leave their new homes and return to friendlier settlements.

Though scientists and historians have long debated whether the Vikings spent much time in North America, one fact remains true. People have discovered remains of Viking relics in a number of sites in Newfoundland. The Vikings can definitely claim to be the first Europeans to land in North America, almost 500 years before Christopher Columbus.

 # Exploring Canada

Name: _____

Vikings - Warriors and Explorers

Read the Information Card entitled "Vikings - Warriors and Explorers"

Complete the following activities.

1. Where did the Vikings come from?

   _____
   _____
   _____

2. Why do you think the Vikings kept on searching for new lands to explore? Try to think of three very good reasons.

   _____
   _____
   _____
   _____
   _____

3. Obtain a map of the world from your teacher and mark the route the Vikings may have taken in their explorations, according to the information sheet.

4. Why did the Vikings enjoy their short stay in Vinland?

   _____
   _____
   _____
   _____

5. What reasons may have caused the Vikings to leave Vinland, other than the fact that they did not get along with the Natives?

   _____
   _____
   _____
   _____
   _____
   _____

Exploring Canada

Jacques Cartier and the Settlers From France

In the year 1534, a Frenchman named Jacques Cartier received permission from the King of France to look for a route to the Orient. The Europeans were eager to find a quicker way to India and China where they traded for rare spices, silks and other treasured goods. The King would help pay for the trip and would receive part of the "treasure" that, hopefully, Cartier would bring back.

However, Cartier did not reach the Orient. Instead, he sailed into the area of Prince Edward Island, on Canada's east coast. The Natives were friendly and when he returned to France with news of his discovery, two of the chief's sons went with him.

The following year Cartier decided to follow the information that the Natives had given him and search for a land "of great wealth" which they called the Saguenay. Though he journeyed far down the St. Lawrence River to a place known as Hochelaga by the Natives (present day Montréal) he did not find the "kingdom of riches".

His last trip to the New World took place in 1541. Cartier came with five ships and some colonists, many of whom were convicts. He was determined to find gold. After a very harsh winter in the area of Stadacona (present day Québec City), Cartier returned to France with an exciting discovery. He had found gold.

His excitement soon turned to bitter disappointment when it was discovered that all he had found was iron pyrite or "fool's gold". France soon lost interest in exploring this New World and it would be almost sixty years before colonists would again set up homes in Canada. The only French visitors to the area would be fishermen stopping to trade with the Natives before heading back to France with their catch of cod and haddock.

 # Exploring Canada

Name: _____

Jacques Cartier and the Settlers From France

Read the Information Card entitled "Jacques Cartier and the Settlers From France".

Answer the following questions with complete sentence answers.

1. For what reasons did Cartier wish to explore the area known as the New World?

   _____
   _____
   _____
   _____
   _____

2. The Natives said that the land of Saguenay had great riches but Cartier found none. What might the Natives have been talking about?

   _____
   _____
   _____
   _____

3. After Cartier left, for a long time only French fishermen came to the New World. Why?

   _____
   _____
   _____
   _____

4. How might Cartier have tried to get the French king interested in letting him go back to the New World? Pretend you were his friend and had given him some suggestions. What suggestions would you make?

   _____
   _____
   _____
   _____
   _____

Exploring Canada

Samuel de Champlain and the Settlers From France

In 1603 another Frenchman named Champlain made his first visit to Canada or New France. Over the next few years, as a member of several French fur trading expeditions, he explored a large portion of the area we know today as New Brunswick and Nova Scotia. Despite several harsh winters, which saw some of the colonists die of scurvy, it was the cancellation of the fur-trading monopoly that forced the French explorer and his companions to return to France.

However, Champlain soon returned to New France and convinced the leader of the expedition to build a settlement on the St. Lawrence River. Champlain said that the site (presently Québec City) would be easier to defend against their enemies, the English, and would also give them an easier route into the interior of New France. You must remember that the government of France did not want to settle people in the New World to farm, but rather to hunt for furs that would be sent to France.

Champlain made a number of trips into the interior of the new country. One, in the summer of 1615, covered a distance of 90 kilometres. It took 22 days to travel along the Ottawa River by canoe, and then by land and water to Lake Huron, then south below Lake Ontario and into the territory controlled by the Iroquois.

Though Champlain and his fellow explorers wound up in a fight with the Iroquois, he still was able to make many records and maps of his journeys that would help later explorers travel the interior of the New World.

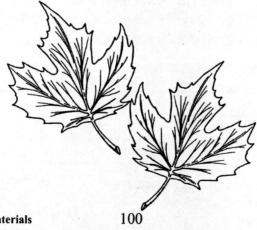

 # Exploring Canada

Name: _____

Samuel de Champlain and the Settlers From France

Read the Information Card entitled "Samuel de Champlain and the Settlers From France".

Answer the following questions with complete sentence answers.

1. Many of the men who went with Champlain to New France suffered from scurvy and often died. What is scurvy? Is there a cure?

   _____
   _____
   _____

2. Why did Champlain feel that the site at Québec City would be a good one for the French explorers to use as a base?

   _____
   _____
   _____

3. What problems or difficulties might Champlain have experienced on his 90 kilometre journey in 1615?

   _____
   _____
   _____

4. For what reasons did Champlain make so many trips throughout the territory of New France?

   _____
   _____
   _____

5. Why do you think the Iroquois were so angry at seeing Champlain and his men? Do you agree or disagree with their feelings? Why?

   _____
   _____
   _____

6. How would Champlain's maps of New France help later explorers?

   _____
   _____
   _____

The Colonizing of New France

As the fur trade expanded, the French soon realized that settlers could be useful in establishing outposts for their fur traders whom they called "Coureurs de Bois". The settlements of Stadacona and Hochelaga grew as French settlers were brought by ship to develop farms.

The King of France owned all the land in the new colony and he granted large sections of it to important individuals such as church leaders, army officers, or people in the government. These people were the "seigneurs". They in turn were expected to sub-divide their sections of land, "seigneuries", into smaller lots, "rotures", which were granted to the peasant farmers. These farmers were called "censitaires" or more commonly in New France, "habitants". The seigneur kept one section of the seigneury for his own farm. This was called the "demesne".

The seigneur and censitaire had certain obligations under the seigneurial system. The seigneur was to grant land to the censitaires, keep a record of its upkeep, and help to pay for the cost of building a church and the building of roads and bridges. The censitaires had to pay the seigneur taxes and they were required to work on the seigneur's land three or four days a year. The censitaire was supposed to build a house on the roture (land) to live in and he had to cultivate the land and harvest the crops.

Life in New France was very difficult and the settlements grew gradually. The winters were harsh and many settlers died from a disease called "scurvy" when they ran out of fresh meat and vegetables. Some of the early settlements experienced difficulty with the Natives. They were often attacked and killed and their settlements were destroyed by the Native tribes. The Native people did not like the growing number of colonists taking over the lands that had belonged to them for thousands of years.

The French colonists did not like English colonists settling in North America along the Atlantic coast. France and England were both competing for the fish and furs found in North America. Tensions grew between the two countries as French ships were frequently being attacked by English ships.

 # Exploring Canada

Name: _____

The Colonizing of New France

Read the Information Card entitled "The Colonizing of New France".

Answer the following questions with complete sentences.

1. Why did the French government finally allow settlers to come to New France?
   _____
   _____
   _____

2. What is a seigneury? Who granted seigneuries to certain people?
   _____
   _____
   _____

3. What was the Seigneur's duties?
   _____
   _____
   _____

4. What was the censitaire's duties?
   _____
   _____
   _____
   _____

5. What were some of the problems experienced by the French colonists in New France?
   _____
   _____
   _____
   _____

Exploring Canada

The Fight Over Fur!

As the demand for fur pelts in Europe grew, so did the number of people interested in hunting fur-bearing animals. The Europeans wanted fur for hats, gloves and, of course, coats. The French were kept busy supplying this demand. Naturally other countries were interested in the wealth of the New World.

The English and Dutch had also set up colonies in the New World but south of the French settlements. The Dutch eventually left the area and the English established claim over an area they called the Thirteen Colonies. This area includes most of what is known as the Eastern United States.

An English fur-trading company known as the Hudson's Bay Company was established in 1670 and began trapping furs in the Thirteen Colonies and beyond. This company set up fur-trading posts, beginning with two on the Hudson Bay and James Bay coastlines. The Natives were encouraged to bring any furs they trapped to these trading posts. The results were excellent and the Hudson's Bay Company expanded their trading posts until they were in direct competition with the fur-traders of New France.

Despite a treaty signed by the French and English that divided up the New World into specific areas where each could build fur-trading posts, the peace between the two countries did not last long.

By the spring of 1759 the English, in a number of battles, were able to gradually gain control over all the French trading posts and forts (built to protect these posts). The town that represented the heart of New France, however, was Québec City. The English knew that capturing Québec City would mean the end of French control in the New World.

Under the leadership of General Wolfe, the English troops attacked and captured the Québec City in September 1759. It would be, however, another four years before peace was finally declared between the French and the English.

After the peace settlement, the English reduced the huge borders of New France in an effort to control its newest colony. They allowed the French colonists to retain their own language and religion. Later the borders of Québec (the new colony's name) were allowed to expand. This annoyed the settlers in the Thirteen Colonies.

When the American Revolution began in the Thirteen Colonies, people who supported the English government decided to leave that area and head north to the areas known as the Maritime Provinces as well as Québec and Ontario. From 1778 on, the Loyalists, as they were called, helped the new colony in the north grow in size and strength.

 # Exploring Canada

Name: _____

The Fight Over Fur!

Read the Information Card entitled "The Fight Over Fur!"

1. Why did the Europeans want to bring so much fur in from the New World?

   _____
   _____
   _____

2. What is a "pelt"?

   _____
   _____
   _____

3. What types of fur do you think the Europeans bought from the fur traders of New France?

   _____
   _____
   _____

4. The Hudson's Bay Company is the oldest company (store) in the world. It was founded in 1670. How old is it today?

   _____
   _____
   _____

5. Why did the French and English end up fighting each other? Who won? Why do you think they couldn't settle their problems peacefully?

   _____
   _____
   _____
   _____
   _____

6. Who were the Loyalists? Why do you think they felt comfortable coming to Canada?

   _____
   _____
   _____

Changes in the New Colony

After the American Revolution there were many changes in the young British colony to the north. The area referred to as Upper Canada (Ontario) began to increase its population thanks to many Loyalists coming from the United States.

Within a few years the New American nation was facing many difficulties with Great Britain. In an effort to establish control in North America the Americans decided to attack Canada.

The Americans felt that if they were able to conquer Upper and Lower Canada they would be able to show the British Government that they were not a small country that could be pushed around.

From 1812 to 1814, many battles were fought between the troops of Lower and Upper Canada and those of the American army. It was a war that nobody really won. Despite losses on both sides, peace negotiators decided that all territories won and lost would return to the original holders.

The peace settlement included the decision that the boundary from the Great Lakes to the Rocky Mountains would be the 49th Parallel.

The War of 1812 made the people of Upper and Lower Canada feel like they were part of a real country, united together. This was an important step towards eventually wanting to become a country! The small British colony was on the road towards becoming a nation.

 # Exploring Canada

Name: _____

Changes in the New Colony

Read the Information Card entitled "Changes in the New Colony".

Complete the following activities.

1. What is Upper Canada known as today?

   _____
   _____
   _____
   _____

2. What is Lower Canada known as today?

   _____
   _____
   _____
   _____

3. Why did the Americans decide to attack Canada?

   _____
   _____
   _____
   _____

4. What would a "peace negotiator" have to do?

   _____
   _____
   _____
   _____

5. Today the line that divides Canada and the United States is called "the longest undefended border in the world". What does this mean?

   _____
   _____
   _____
   _____
   _____

Confederation Comes to Canada

The colony of Canada had many problems to overcome before it was eventually granted the privilege of establishing a Confederation of provinces.

During the Rebellions of 1837, many people openly showed their dislike of the way the British government was running its North American colony. The British were naturally afraid that they would lose what was left of a profitable segment of their Empire, and quickly sent Lord Durham to help solve the problems.

The population of Upper Canada was growing very fast by colonial standards. The town of York (Toronto) had grown from 700 people in 1815 to over 30 000 by 1851. The colony needed new roads, more schools and a better form of local government to keep pace with its rapid growth.

By the 1860s, the Canadas were ready to apply for permission to become a nation. The inhabitants didn't want to separate from Great Britain, like the Americans, but they did want to have control over the running of their country. They wanted to collect taxes and keep the money in Canada so that they could build roads, guard their borders and make decisions that affected the people living in Canada.

In 1864, at the Charlottetown Conference, ideas were discussed and written down. Representatives from Canada were sent to Britain to request permission to form a Confederation of provinces to be known as the Dominion of Canada. Permission was granted.

On July 1, 1867 the Dominion of Canada was born! It consisted of four provinces: Ontario, Québec, New Brunswick and Nova Scotia. Strangely enough, Prince Edward Island, the site of the Charlottetown Conference, did not enter Confederation at that time but waited several years before doing so!

The British monarch at that time, Queen Victoria, had decided that Ottawa would be the capital of the colony of the Canadas back in 1857. It was an obvious choice then that it should also become the capital of the new nation. Work had already begun on the construction of the Parliament Buildings for the colonies, so there was also a practical reason for choosing to keep the capital city of the new nation in Ottawa. Canada entered a new period in her growth; a nation at last!

 # Exploring Canada

Name: _____

Confederation Comes to Canada

Read the Information Cards entitled "Confederation Comes to Canada".

Answer the following questions with complete sentences.

1. In 1837 Canada had two rebellions, one in Upper Canada, one in Lower Canada. Why did they happen?

   _____
   _____
   _____
   _____

2. What were some of the things the colony of the Canadas needed?

   _____
   _____
   _____
   _____

3. Why do you think Ottawa had been picked originally as a capital for the colonies of Upper and Lower Canada?

   _____
   _____
   _____
   _____

4. Canada Day celebrates the founding of the Dominion of Canada. When is it held?

   _____
   _____

5. For what practical reason was Ottawa chosen as the site for Canada's new capital city?

   _____
   _____
   _____
   _____

The Young Nation Grows

In 1869 Canada purchased land known as Rupert's Land and also the area known as the Northwest Territories from the Hudson's Bay Company. Within three years, the provinces of Manitoba and British Columbia joined the Confederation and, in 1873, Prince Edward Island also voted to join.

Canadian politicians promised the people of British Columbia to build a railroad if British Columbia joined the Canadian Confederation. This colony on the west coast needed an efficient way of shipping goods from eastern Canada. Many politicians in Ottawa feared that if the railway was not built soon then British Columbia might turn to her nearest neighbour, the United States, for help. Canada did not want to lose the valuable harbours of the west coast or the potential resources of British Columbia!

In 1885, the work on the transcontinental railway was finally finished. At a point in the Selkirk Mountains called Craigellachie, Donald Smith, president of the railway, drove in "the last spike" marking the completion of the railway.

By 1890, the east and west coasts of Canada were also linked by telegraph wire. Railroad stations were also used as telegraph offices and the telegraph wires rang alongside the railroad. The railways still run the telegraph system today.

 # Exploring Canada

Name: _____

The Young Nation Grows

Read the Information Card entitled "The Young Nation Grows".

Answer the following questions with complete sentences.

1. Using a resource book on Canada from your library or the internet, find out when the provinces of Manitoba and British Columbia joined the Confederation.

   _____
   _____
   _____

2. Why do you think that Prince Edward Island waited until 1873 to join Canada?

   _____
   _____

3. Why did the Canadian government promise to build a railroad to British Columbia if that area joined in the Canadian Confederation?

   _____
   _____

4. The driving in of the "last spike" is a famous picture in many Canadian history books. Who else was responsible for getting the railroad built? Use a resource book from your library to find the answer?

   _____
   _____
   _____

5. Why would it be important for the telegraph wire to be linked up across the country?

   _____
   _____

6. What advantage would there be in having the telegraph wires follow the railway lines?

   _____
   _____
   _____

Problems in Western Canada

With the addition of new settlers into the western areas of Canada, the government decided that a group of law enforcement officers should be established so that the territories and provinces would receive protection from anyone who decided to break the law.

The North West Mounted Police was established in 1873 and set up "offices" in many parts of Western Canada. The "Mounties" were recognized by their distinctive red and black uniforms and gradually became a symbol of Canada's growth and heritage.

In 1870, the Natives and Métis rebelled against the Canadian Government. They felt that the new nation was destroying their hunting grounds and "trespassing on their property". The rebellion, led by a Métis leader named Louis Riel, was soon stopped. In 1885, Louis Riel again led a rebellion. This time both the Canadian army and the North West Mounted Police were called in to help. Louis Riel was captured, put on trial and eventually executed for his part in the rebellion. The Natives and Métis were forced to accept the big changes that were happening to their land because of the coming of the settlers and the railroad.

 # Exploring Canada

Name: _____

Problems in Western Canada

Read the Information Card entitled "Problems in Western Canada".

Answer the following questions with complete sentences.

1. The North West Mounted Police eventually had their name changed to the Royal Canadian Mounted Police (R.C.M.P.). Describe their uniform. Use a resource book from the library or the internet to help you.

   _____
   _____
   _____
   _____
   _____

2. Who are the Métis?

   _____
   _____
   _____

3. Why did the Natives and Métis fight the government of Canada in two different rebellions? Do you agree with their reasons for fighting? Why?

   _____
   _____
   _____
   _____
   _____

4. "The railway solved many problems but started more as well". What does this statement mean?

   _____
   _____
   _____
   _____

 # Exploring Canada

Into the Twentieth Century

By 1900, the population of Canada had reached over seven million people. Though this seems to be small, it was indeed a large number for a young nation.

With more and more settlers swelling the population of the western territories, two more provinces were created: Alberta and Saskatchewan. It would be many more years before the last province would eventually join the partnership begun in 1867.

Many industries were being established, especially in the provinces of Ontario and Québec. It was good that Canada was beginning to make more things in the country instead of bringing those products in from other countries.

One of the biggest industries, the pulp and paper industry, soon found that the rest of the world wanted lots of Canada's timber resources. The logging industry was kept very busy supplying this demand.

Making farm machinery, mining for gold and other minerals, as well as the building of new steel mills, were all industries that were growing rapidly in Canada. These things are usually considered the signs of a good, healthy economy. It meant Canada was able to support itself quite well and did not have to turn to Great Britain for help.

Back in 1872, trade unions were made legal in Canada. Though people still worked long hours and for small wages, gradually the unions were helping the workers to receive more money for the work they did.

Women in Canada made up one seventh of the workforce by 1900, yet they were given little pay and were not considered to have the same rights as men! Few women were allowed to be educated beyond elementary school and it wasn't until 1887 that the first woman was allowed to enrol in the University of Toronto. Within ten years, however, over one third of the students there were women. Still, it would not be until 1920 that women in Canada would be given the right to vote.

Posters were put up all over Europe and other parts of the world encouraging people to come to Canada. It was important to the Canadian government to continue to attract new settlers to Canada so that industries and farms would continue to receive the workers they needed to operate and grow bigger. Immigrants from every corner of the world came to Canada. Today the "cultural mosiac" of Canada has continued to develop. Different cultures have added to Canada's growth and development as a nation.

Exploring Canada

Name: _____

Into the Twentieth Century

Read the Information Card entitled "Into the Twentieth Century".

Answer the following questions with complete sentences.

1. Canada's population in 1900 was seven million. What is its population today? Compare today's population in Canada to that of Russia, the United States, Great Britain, China and Japan. Where does Canada stand?

   _____
   _____
   _____
   _____

2. What are some of the resources found in Canada that the rest of the world wants to buy?

   _____
   _____
   _____

3. How did trade unions help the workers?

   _____
   _____
   _____

4. Why do you think women eventually were given the right to vote in elections?

   _____
   _____
   _____

5. What do the words "cultural mosaic" mean?

   _____
   _____
   _____

6. Why was it important for the government to keep trying to get people from other countries to come to live in Canada?

   _____
   _____

Exploring Canada

Canada and the World

Two of Canada's early prime ministers worked hard to get Canada recognized as a "world nation". John A. Macdonald and Wilfrid Laurier were determined that Canada would not be viewed as a colony of Britain. Macdonald began encouraging immigrants to come to Canada and even set up ways of protecting Canadian products from cheaper American-made goods. Laurier took a stand against the British government when they asked the colonies for money to support a British navy. Laurier refused, saying that Canada would build her own navy and could be able to help Britain whenever necessary.

Canada fought with Britian in three important wars: The Boer War of 1899, World War I (1914 - 1918) and World War II (1939 - 1945). Canada's participation in these three conflicts helped to develop her sense of identity as a nation. Wars are very sad and terrifying experiences but historians say that they often help a country experience a "togetherness" feeling that is necessary if people are to work together to build a country.

There were other events in the twentieth century that helped Canada see herself as a growing nation. The beginning of a national airline company to link the major cities of Canada and the establishing of a national radio and then television network helped Canadians keep in contact with their own and other countries' developments.

In 1949, the tenth and final province joined the Canadian confederation. With its announcement, Newfoundland made Canada truly a nation speading from sea to sea!

When Canada celebrated its first one hundred years as a nation in 1967 the event was marked with huge celebrations, pageants and Expo '67. In 1976 Canada hosted the Summer Olympics and in 1988 she played host to the Winter Olympic Games. Both these events showed the world that Canada was indeed a strong world nation.

When the British government established a Commonwealth of Nations in 1931, Canada became recognized as a nation and was no longer thought of as a colony of Britain.

Canadians are proud of their history and heritage. They established a country using democratic procedures in 1867 and helped Canada to grow into a world-class nation where many people from all over the world have come to live and eventually call Canada "home".

 # Exploring Canada

Name: _____

Canada and the World

Read the Information Card called "Canada and the World".

Complete the following activities.

1. How did Macdonald and Laurier try to get Canada recognized as an important country in the world?

   _____

   _____

   _____

   _____

2. Wars can cause some good things to happen. What did it say in "Canada and the World" information card? Can you think of any other "good results" of a war? Ask an adult for his or her opinion and record it.

   _____

   _____

   _____

   _____

   _____

   _____

   _____

   _____

3. Why do you think it took Newfoundland so long to join Canada?

   _____

   _____

   _____

   _____

4. Using a reference or resource book find the cities in which the following "world events" took place in Canada:

   a) Expo '67 _____

   b) Olympic Games in 1976 (Summer)_____

   c) Olympic Games in 1988 (Winter) _____

5. Canada finally stopped being considered as a colony of Britian in 1931. Why do you think that Great Britian decided to form a Commonwealth of Nations where all her former colonies would be seen as independent countries?

_____
_____
_____
_____
_____
_____

6. Canada's flag is quite unique. Find a picture of it and make a duplicate of it by yourself. When was this flag adopted as the official flag of Canada?

_____
_____

Name: _____

Where is Canada?

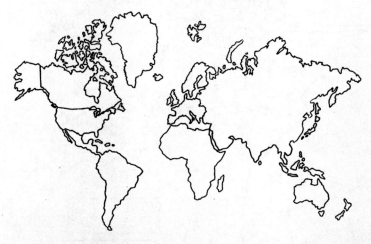

Canada is the _____ largest country in the world. It covers the _____ half of the continent called _____ except for Alaska. It shares this continent with the _____ and _____. Canada is _____ square kilometres in area. _____ is larger than Canada.

What is a continent? _____
_____

What is an ocean? _____
_____

Using the map provided, label the continents and oceans.

The seven continents found in the world are:

1._____   5._____
2._____   6._____
3._____   7._____
4._____

The four oceans found in the world are:

1._____   3._____
2._____   4._____

Exploring Canada

Name: _____

Canada's Borders

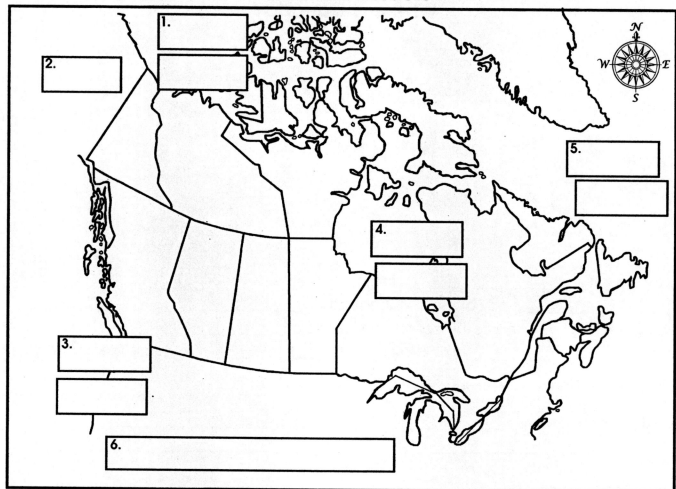

1. What is a border? _____
   _____
   _____
   _____

2. In the west, Canada borders on the _____ and _____ .

3. In the east, Canada borders on the _____ .

4. In the north, Canada borders on the _____
   and _____ .

5. In the south, Canada borders on the _____ .

6. Into how many areas has Canada been divided? _____

7. Are the areas all the same size? _____

8. How many areas are bordered by water? _____

9. How many areas are bordered by other land areas? _____

Exploring Canada

Name: _____

Canada's Provinces and Territories

1. Canada has _____ provinces and three _____.

2. The names of Canada's provinces and territories are listed on the flag. Can you write their names in the correct alphabetical order.

_____
_____
_____
_____
_____
_____
_____
_____
_____
_____
_____
_____
_____

Nunavut
Ontario
Alberta
Manitoba
Newfoundland & Labrador
Québec
Nova Scotia
Yukon Territory
Saskatchewan
British Columbia
Northwest Territories
Prince Edward Island
New Brunswick

3. Which province is an island? _____

4. Write the names of the Atlantic Provinces.

_____
_____

5. Write the names of the Prairie Provinces.

_____

6. Write the names of the territories.

_____

7. Using the map provided, correctly label "Canada's Provinces and Territories". Using the map provided, correctly label "Canada's Capital Cities" for each province and territory.

Exploring Canada

Name: _____

Let's Research Canada

1. Which territory in Canada is the largest? _____

2. Which province in Canada is the largest? _____

3. Which province is an island? _____

4. In which capital city will you find the largest shopping mall in Canada? _____

5. Which two capital cities are named after Queen Victoria? _____

6. In which provinces are the Rocky Mountains located? _____

7. Which capital city is known as "The Crossroads City"? _____

8. Which capital city has the largest population? _____

9. What is the floral emblem for Ontario? _____

10. Which territory has two very large lakes? _____

11. Which province has one of the Seven Wonders of the World? _____

12. Which capital city is the only walled city in North America outside Mexico?

    _____

13. In which province will you find the flowerpot rocks? _____

14. In which province did the heroine of Lucy Maud Montgomery's classic story live?

    _____

15. In which province would you find Peggy's Cove? _____

16. Which province has chosen the Puffin as its provincial bird? _____

17. In which capital city will you find Province House, the birthplace of Canada?

    _____

18. Which capital city is located on the Saint John River? _____

19. Which island province is now connected to the mainland of Canada with a long

    bridge? _____

20. In which province would you find totem poles? _____

Name: _____

Physical Regions of Canada

Physical Region: _____

Location	Land Forms	Minerals	Vegetation	Wildlife

Physical Region: _____

Location	Land Forms	Minerals	Vegetation	Wildlife

Physical Region: _____

Location	Land Forms	Minerals	Vegetation	Wildlife

Exploring Canada

Name: _____

Important Rivers of Canada

1. Name three rivers that are tributaries of the St. Lawrence River.

    _____

    _____

2. Name four rivers that flow into James Bay.

    _____

    _____

3. Name four rivers that flow into Hudson Bay.

    _____

    _____

4. Which river has its source at Lake Ontario and its mouth at the Atlantic Ocean?

    _____

5. Name two rivers that flow into the Pacific Ocean.

    _____

6. Which two rivers flow through the three prairie provinces?

    _____

7. Name four rivers that flow north and empty into the Arctic Ocean.

    _____

    _____

8. Name the river whose name is the same as a territory.

    _____

9. On a map provided, trace in blue all the rivers.

10. On a map provided, circle in green the names of four rivers not entirely in Canada.

11. On a map provided, underline in red the names of the rivers in your province or territory. Their names are:

    _____

    _____

    _____

    _____

Exploring Canada

Name: _____

How Long Are the Rivers of Canada?

There are many freshwater rivers in Canada. Each river is a different length. On the chart below arrange the names of Canada's Rivers from the largest to the smallest.

Canadian Rivers

Laird River 1 115
Fraser River 1 370
Yukon River 3 185
Athabasca River 1 231

St. Lawrence River 3 058
Churchill River 1 609
Mackenzie River 4 241

Ottawa River 1 271
Peace River 1 923
Columbia River 2 000

Name of River	Length in Kilometres	Flows Into
1.		
2.		
3.		
4.		
5.		
6.		
7.		
8.		
9.		
10.		

Exploring Canada

Name: _____

Rivers and Lakes of Canada

1. Using an atlas, locate the provinces and territories in which the following rivers are found.

   a) Saguenay River _____

   b) Trent River _____

   c) Madawaska River _____

   d) Abitibi River _____

   e) Peace River _____

   f) Fraser River _____

   g) Nelson River _____

   h) Saskatchewan River _____

   i) Detroit River _____

   j) St. Maurice River _____

   k) Ottawa River _____

   l) St. Clair River _____

   m) Slave River _____

   n) Skeena River _____

   o) Thames River _____

   p) Stikine River _____

   q) Qu'Appele River _____

   r) Thompson River _____

   s) Saint John River _____

   t) Gander River _____

Exploring Canada

2. Using an atlas locate the provinces and territories in which the following lakes are found. Classify each lake according to its province on this sheet.

Lake Louise	**Lake Simcoe**	**Lake Huron**	**Lake Winnipeg**
Lake Nipissing	**Great Slave Lake**	**Lake Nipigon**	**Lake of the Woods**
Lake Athabasca	**Great Bear Lake**	**Lake St. John**	**Lake Abitibi**
Lake St. Clair	**Lake Winnipegosis**	**Grand Lake**	**Lake Mistassini**
Lake Garry	**Smallwood Reservoir**	**Lake Aberdeen**	**Reindeer Lake**
Kootenay Lake	**Lake Okanagan**	**Lake Ontario**	**Lake Erie**

a) Newfoundland & Labrador:_____

_____

b) Québec: _____

_____

c) Ontario: _____

_____

_____

_____

d) Manitoba: _____

_____

e) Saskatchewan: _____

_____

f) Alberta: _____

_____

g) British Columbia: _____

_____

h) New Brunswick: _____

_____

i) Nunavut: _____

j) Northwest Territories:_____

_____

 # Exploring Canada

Name: _____

The Population of Canada

1. Canada is the _____ largest country in the world with nearly
_____ _____ square kilometres of land. Its population is almost
_____ _____ . About 75 percent of the people live within 150
kilometres of the southern border. Much of Canada is _____ because
the country's terrain is _____ and its climate is quite _____
in northern areas.

2. Listed below are the names of the provinces and territories and their populations.
Complete the empty chart by listing the provinces and territories according to
population from the smallest to the largest. (Note: Population figure from 1999
Census.)

Province/Territory	Population	Province/Territory	Population
Newfoundland & Labrador	533 700	_____	_____
Prince Edward Island	138 500	_____	_____
New Brunswick	757 000	_____	_____
Nova Scotia	942 600	_____	_____
Québec	7 410 500	_____	_____
Ontario	11 874 400	_____	_____
Manitoba	1 150 000	_____	_____
Saskatchewan	1 015 700	_____	_____
Alberta	3 064 200	_____	_____
British Columbia	4 095 900	_____	_____
Yukon Territory	29 800	_____	_____
Northwest Territories	40 800	_____	_____
Nunavut	28 100	_____	_____

Exploring Canada

Name: _____

Natural Vegetation Regions

Throughout Canada different types of vegetation are able to grow. Canada's varied climate affects the type of vegetation found in certain areas.

Examine the map entitled **"Natural Vegetation Regions of Canada"**.

Locate the answers to the following questions.

1. What types of trees grow in Newfoundland? _____

2. What types of vegetation grow above the treeline?
   _____

3. In which province are the trees tall and the forests dense? _____

4. Which provinces have grasslands?
   _____

5. In which territories and provinces would you find tundra?
   _____
   _____

6. In which provinces would you find deciduous trees growing?
   _____
   _____

7. Which provinces and territory have a variety of things growing in the mountains?
   _____
   _____

8. What is a coniferous tree? _____
   _____

   Name three coniferous trees that grow in Canada. _____
   _____

9. What is a deciduous tree? _____
   _____

   Name three deciduous trees that grow in Canada. _____
   _____

10. What is tundra? _____
    _____

Natural Vegetation Regions of Canada

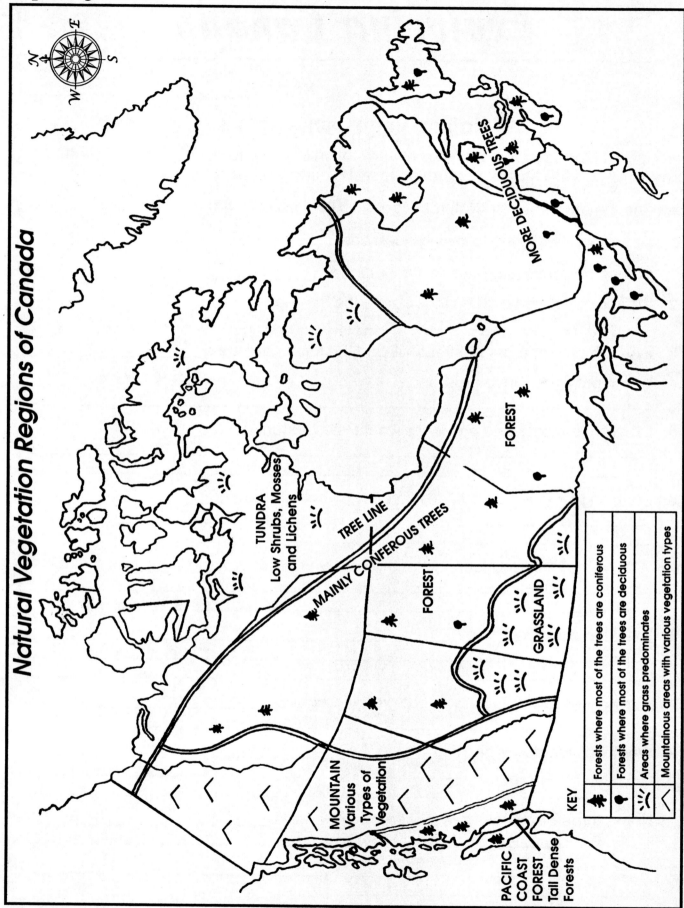

MORE DECIDUOUS TREES

FOREST

TUNDRA
Low Shrubs, Mosses
and Lichens

TREE LINE

MAINLY CONIFEROUS TREES

FOREST

GRASSLAND

MOUNTAIN
Various
Types of
Vegetation

PACIFIC
COAST
FOREST
Tall Dense
Forests

KEY

Forests where most of the trees are coniferous

Forests where most of the trees are deciduous

Areas where grass predominates

Mountainous areas with various vegetation types

 # Exploring Canada

Canada's Government

A government is the machinery set up by individuals to enable them to do what others cannot do on their own. Without some form of government there would be no order or protection for people and their property. A government's basic task is to make a set of laws to allow people in a society to live together in peace and security. A government also makes sure laws are obeyed and sets up punishments or penalties that protect the interests of the people as a whole against the greed or ambition of any one person or any one group.

There are many different kinds of governments but they all carry out three main tasks or functions. They are legislative, executive and judicial. The legislative function is the making of laws or the passing of legislation. The executive function is putting the laws into effect on a daily basis. The judicial function is to decide if an individual has broken society's laws and to punish the guilty.

The government of Canada has been described as a democracy, a monarchy, a parliamentary system, a cabinet government, and a federal government.

The word democracy comes from two Greek words: *demos*, which means *people* and *kratos* which means *power.* A democracy is a system of government in which the people rule or have the power.

Canada is considered a democracy because of the way that we choose our government or rulers. In a modern country, democracy means a system in which the citizens of the country freely choose the people who will govern them. In Canada we elect others to represent us in governing the country and we sometimes describe this system as a representative government.

Canada's government has also been described as a monarchy. In a monarchy, the monarch is the source of all authority. Queen Elizabeth II is the Queen of Canada. She is represented by the Governor-General. Neither the Queen nor the Governor-General plays a major role in the actual government of Canada.

Canada's government has also been described as a parliamentary government. Canada's parliament consists of the Queen represented by the Governor-General, the Senate, whose members are appointed and the House of Commons, made up of representatives elected by the Canadian voters. Parliamentary government in Canada means government by Queen, Senate and the House of Commons.

Our system of government has also been referred to as a cabinet government. The Cabinet ministers carry out the executive functions of the government. Cabinet ministers must be elected to the House of Commons or have seats in the Senate. In order to stay in office they must have support of a majority of the members of the House of Commons. The Cabinet ministers - the executive branch of government - are responsible to the

House of Commons - the legislative branch. The House of Commons is in turn elected by the people and responsible to them. Our government has a line of responsibility running from the bottom to the top and because of this responsibility, Canadians sometimes use the term responsible government to describe our system.

People often refer to our government as a federal system of government. This means our government has a system in which the power to make laws is shared between two levels of government - a national or central government and provincial governments. Canada is a federation of provinces and territories with both federal and provincial governments, because both levels of government have the power to make laws.

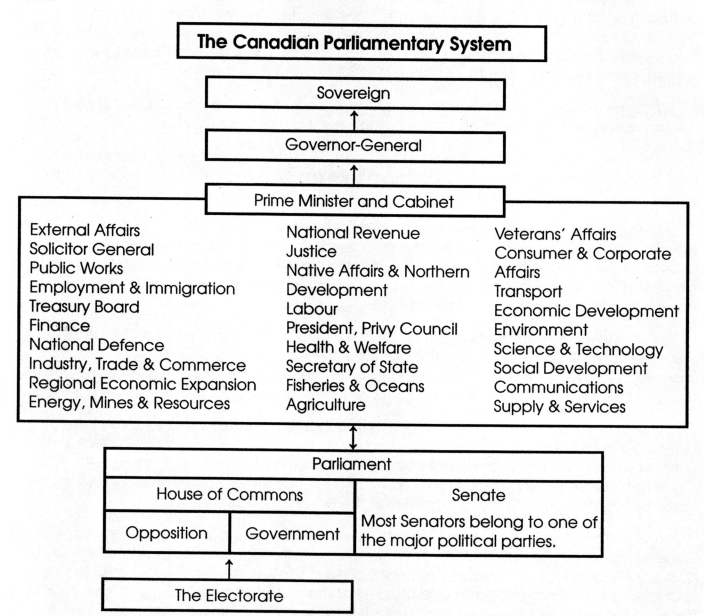

The Canadian Parliamentary System

Sovereign

Governor-General

Prime Minister and Cabinet

External Affairs	National Revenue	Veterans' Affairs
Solicitor General	Justice	Consumer & Corporate
Public Works	Native Affairs & Northern	Affairs
Employment & Immigration	Development	Transport
Treasury Board	Labour	Economic Development
Finance	President, Privy Council	Environment
National Defence	Health & Welfare	Science & Technology
Industry, Trade & Commerce	Secretary of State	Social Development
Regional Economic Expansion	Fisheries & Oceans	Communications
Energy, Mines & Resources	Agriculture	Supply & Services

Parliament

House of Commons		Senate
Opposition	Government	Most Senators belong to one of the major political parties.

The Electorate

Exploring Canada

Canadian Executive Offices - The Governor-General

The Governor-General is an appointed official who represents the Queen usually for five years. The Prime Minister of Canada recommends a candidate for this office and the Queen appoints the person to represent her in Canada.

At one time, the Governor-General had a great deal of power and was always from the United Kingdom (Britain). In 1952, Vincent Massey was the first Canadian appointed to this position. Today, the Governor-General has very little power. He or she represents the Queen but follows the direction and advice of the cabinet. The Governor-General entertains important foreign visitors and honours distinguished Canadians, cuts ribbons to open hospitals and art galleries and lends support to many worthy causes and events. These duties free up the Prime Minister to concentrate on running the country.

The most important role of the office of Governor-General is that is serves as a reminder of our past. The opening of every session of Parliament is crammed with history, pomp and ceremony. The Governor-General arrives at the Parliament Buildings in a special carriage and then there is a grand procession to the Senate Chamber. The members of the House of commons are invited to stand at the bar of the door to the Senate and listen to the Speech from the Throne, read by the Governor-General.

The Governor-General resides at a large mansion in Ottawa called Rideau Hall.

The Prime Minister

The head or leader of the Canadian government is the prime minister. He/She is the leader of the majority party in the House of Commons and is directly elected by the people. The office of the prime minister has no fixed term. However, general elections are held every five years.

Sir. John A. Macdonald

The prime minister is then appointed by the Governor-General and follows the wishes of the majority in the House of Commons. He/She holds office only with the backing of this majority. If a prime minister loses this support through a vote of no confidence by the House of Commons, he/she must either resign or request the Governor-General to call a new general election.

The office and duties of Canada's prime minister are based on those of the British prime minister. He/She is the leader of the House of Commons and acts as the voice of the nation. He/She directs foreign policy, serves as the leader of the governing party and with the aid of a House leader, guides debates and discussions in the House.

Exploring Canada

The prime minister is the most powerful person in the government. He/She chooses the ministers for his/her cabinet and can also ask any one of them to resign. If the minister refuses, the prime minister advises the Governor-General to remove the minister which is done immediately. Cabinet decisions do not necessarily go by majority vote. A strong prime minister, after having listened to everyone's opinions and advice, simply announces that his or her view is the policy of the government, even if most or all the other ministers are opposed. The ministers who are opposed either resign or accept the Prime Minister's decision.

The prime minister lives in an official residence in Ottawa, Ontario at 24 Sussex Drive. The house is maintained by the Canadian government.

The Cabinet

The prime minister's cabinet is made up of approximately 30 ministers. These ministers are chosen by the prime minister from the majority party in the House of Commons.

The cabinet is a powerful part of our Canadian government. It is important because it is the real executive of the country. The cabinet and the prime minister decide the policies the government will follow. It decides whether to raise or lower taxes, whether the country will be at peace or war, whether to improve airports or whether to increase old-age pensions. It is responsible for all legislation and has the power to make new laws.

Each province must be represented by at least one minister. Larger provinces will normally have more ministers than smaller ones in the cabinet. Each minister is given a portfolio which means that he/she is responsible for a government department. Each minister also has a deputy minister who is a permanent head of the department. These officers are civil servants who are employed by the government. Many times a minister knows very little about the portfolio that he/she has been given. The deputy minister runs the department and provides the minister with information about how the department functions and the problems that they must deal with. Each minister is responsible, answerable and accountable for his/her department to the House of Commons.

The cabinet must work as a team. Every cabinet minister must agree and defend all policies decided whether they totally agree with them or not. If a cabinet minister cannot agree and will not support the cabinet on the issue, he/she may resign or be asked to resign from the cabinet by the prime minister. This team playing is referred to as "the collective responsibility of the Cabinet".

Our Parliament

Parliament consists of the Queen, the Senate and the House of Commons. The Upper House is called the Senate and the Lower House is called the House of Commons. The queen is the formal head of Canada. The Governor General represents her at the federal level of Government and the Lieutenant-Governors represent her at the provincial level.

The Governor-General and Lieutenant-Governor for each province govern through a cabinet, headed by the prime minister (federal level) and the premier (provincial level). If an opposing party during an election wins a clear majority (more than half of the seats) in the House of Commons or the provincial Legislature, the Cabinet resigns and the Governor-General or the Lieutenant-Governor calls on the leader of the victorious party to become prime minister or premier and to form a new cabinet. The prime minister selects his own ministers who are then formally appointed by the Governor-General. In the provincial government, the premier selects his/her ministers and they are appointed by the Lieutenant-Governor.

If no party gets a clear majority during an election, the cabinet that was in office before and during the election has two choices. It can resign or it can stay in office and meet the newly elected House right away. If the Cabinet resigns, the Governor General or Lieutenant-Governor will call on the leader of the largest opposition party to form a cabinet. The peoples' representatives in the newly elected House of Commons will decide whether the "minority" government (one whose own party has fewer than half the seats) shall stay in office or be thrown out in either case.

Sometimes a Cabinet is defeated in the House of Commons on a "motion of censure" or "want of confidence". If this happens, the Cabinet must either resign or ask that Parliament be dissolved and a new election called. If the Cabinet resigns, the Governor-General will then ask the leader of the Opposition to form a new Cabinet.

The Governor-General or Lieutenant-Governor could refuse a request for a new election under very exceptional circumstances. For example, if an election gave no party a clear majority and the prime minister asked for a new election without even allowing the new Parliament to meet, the Governor-General or Lieutenant-Governor may say no. A newly elected Parliament must be allowed to meet to see whether it can transact public business. The Governor-General or Lieutenant-Governor could also refuse the request for a new election if a minority government is easily defeated on a motion of confidence in the first session of a new Parliament, and there is a reasonable possibility that a Government of another party can be formed and get the support of the House of Commons.

Members of Parliament or of a provincial Legislature are normally elected for not more than five years. The prime minister can ask for a new election at any time but in certain circumstances he or she would not get it. The Cabinet has no "term". The Cabinet lasts from the time the prime minister is sworn in until he/she resigns or dies. A re-elected Canadian prime minister or premier does not have to be sworn in all over again.

If the prime minister or premier dies or resigns, the Cabinet comes to an end. A new prime minister or premier must be found by the Governor-General or Lieutenant-Governor at once if the leader's party still has a majority in the House of Commons or the provincial Legislature. A prime minister who resigns cannot advise the Governor-General as to his or her successor unless asked. This applies to a premier as well. The Governor-General or Lieutenant-Governor does not have to follow this advice. If a prime minister or premier resigns because of defeat, the Governor-General must call on the leader of the Opposition to form a Government. If a prime minister or premier dies or resigns for personal reasons, then the Governor-General consults leading members of the majority party as to who will most likely be able to form a Government that can command a majority in the House.

The Governor-General or Lieutenant-Governor then meets with the person he or she has decided has the best chance. The new prime minister will only hold office until the majority party has chosen a new leader in a national or provincial convention. This leader will then be called on to form a Government.

A Cabinet at the national or provincial level is made up of ministers. The number of ministers varies. Today's national Cabinet has about 30 members, although smaller cabinets are becoming increasingly popular. Provincial cabinets vary from ten to 22 ministers. Most ministers at the national and provincial levels have "portfolios" which means that each one is in charge of a particular department such as Finance, Foreign Affairs, Education, Health, the Environment, etc. Each minister is responsible, answerable and accountable to the House of Commons or the provincial Legislature for his or her department.

Some ministers do not have "portfolios". They are "Ministers Without Portfolios" and they are not in charge of any department. Ministers of State may be in charge of a particular section of a department or of a "ministry" which is not a full-fledge department. There are also Secretaries of State who are not full members of the Cabinet.

The Senate

The Senate or Upper House is made up of 104 men and women. Its presiding officer, the Speaker of the Senate, and the Senators are appointed by the Governor General on the recommendation of the prime minister. Usually an appointment to the Senate is given as a reward for service to the country. Senators must retire when they are 75 years old or when they miss two consecutive sessions of Parliament. Senators must be at least 30 years old, have real property worth $4 000.00 free of mortgage, and a net worth of at least $4 000.00. They must reside in the province or territory for which they are appointed.

The Senate can initiate bills, except bills providing for the spending of public money or imposing taxes. It has the right to amend or reject any bill as often as it sees fit. No bill can become law unless it has been passed by the Senate. The Senate very rarely uses these powers, and it seldom rejects a bill passed by the House of Commons. The Senate often makes amendments to bills passed by the House of Commons to simplify or clarify the amendments in it.

The Senate carefully examines each bill passed by the House of Commons, clause by clause. Senators listen to various groups and individuals who would be affected by the bill under review. The Senate is made up of members who have specialized knowledge and long years of legal, business or administrative experience. They are often ex-ministers, ex-premiers of provinces, ex-mayors, important lawyers and experienced farmers.

In recent years, the Senate has taken on a new job. Senators are spending their time investigating important public problems as poverty, unemployment, inflation, the aged, land use, science policies, aboriginal affairs, relations with the United States and the efficiency (or lack of it) of government departments. These investigations and reports have led to positive changes in legislation or government policy. It is cheaper to have the Senate investigate these problems than a royal commission as the Senators are paid and they already have a permanent staff working for them.

 # Exploring Canada

The House of Commons

The House of Commons or Lower House has 301 seats. Members of the House are elected by the people during an election. The members are elected for a five year term unless an election is called earlier. Each member of the House represents a constituency (district) of a province or territory. Members do not have to live in the constituency or in the province that they represent.

Canadian Constituencies (2003)	
Area	**Seats**
Ontario	103
Québec	75
British Columbia	34
Alberta	26
Manitoba	14
Saskatchewan	14
Nova Scotia	11
New Brunswich	10
Newfound and Labrador	7
Prince Edward Island	4
Northwest Territories	1
Nunavut	1
Total	301

The members of the House sit in a chamber decorated in the traditional green found in the British Parliament. A parliament is made up of one or more sessions which begins with a Speech from the Throne made by the Governor-General and ends by being dissolved. Parliament sits about 27 weeks of the year. Sittings start in September, and usually continue until June, with breaks or recesses to permit the House members to work in their regions or ridings.

Each session is organized with an agenda from the beginning when the mace (which represents legislative authority) is placed on the table at the start of the day's sitting until the sitting is adjourned. A regular sitting day always includes routine business, committee reports are presented, documents are recorded, ministers make statements, petitions are presented and bills are introduced.

Most of the sitting is spent with the House debating legislation (laws). The Question Period is the highlight of the sitting day. Ministers must defend the activities of their departments and the policies of the government from the members of the House.

It is the duty of the Speaker of the House to make sure there is an orderly flow of business proceeding through the House of Commons. The Speaker interprets the parliamentary rules to maintain order and to defend the rights and privileges of Parliament, Senators and members of the House, including the right to freedom of speech.

 # Exploring Canada

Name: _____

What is a Government?

Since the beginning of time, society has been ruled by some form of _____.
The word *government* means to _____ _____ in a group. Every group
needs people to _____ and _____ decisions that control the
_____ of the group.

Every form of government contains five common elements.

1. Rules of Conduct: Every _____ of people has _____ to govern
    people's lives. The rules affect the _____ group. Rules are made to
    encourage _____ behaviour and to _____ or _____ bad
    behaviours.

2. Authority: All groups are governed by a _____ _____ or
    _____. In a _____ country the _____ are regarded as
    the _____ source of government authority.

3. Acceptance: A government must be _____ by the people for it to exits.
    The people give the government the _____ to exercise _____.
    The people develop _____ to symbols of the government such as a
    _____ or _____ _____.

4. Jurisdiction: This is the part of the government that has the _____ to make
    and enforce _____ or _____.

5. Law Enforcement: In order for _____ or _____ to have any effect,
    someone has to _____ them. In a society there would be no _____
    if people were allowed to ignore or disobey them.

 # Exploring Canada

Name: _____

What is Canada's Government?

Our government carries out _____ main tasks or functions. They are _____, _____ and _____. The legislative function is to make new _____ and to pass them. The executive function is to make sure the laws are put into _____. The judicial function is to decide if a person has _____ society's laws and to _____ the guilty.

Canada's government has been described as a _____, a _____, a _____ system, a _____ government and a _____ system.

It is a democracy because we _____ the people who _____ us. Sometimes this system is also called a _____ government.

Our government has also been described as a _____ because _____ is the Queen of Canada and is represented by the _____ _____. Neither the Queen nor the Governor General is involved in our government.

Some people refer to our government as a _____ government because Canada's parliament consists of the Queen, represented by the Governor-General, the Senate and the House of Commons. Our government has been fashioned after the _____ _____ in many ways.

Canada's government has often been referred to as a _____ government because the Cabinet ministers carry out the executive functions of the government. The Cabinet ministers are responsible to the _____. The House of Commons is responsible to the _____ who elected its members. This line of responsibility running from the top of the government to the bottom makes our government a _____ one.

People often call our government a _____ system because it has a _____ government and _____ and _____ governments. Canada is a _____ of provinces and territories and it has both a federal and provincial government because both governments have the _____ to make _____.

 # Exploring Canada

Name: _____

Executive Offices

The Governor-General

1. Who is the Governor-General?

   _____

   _____

2. Who does the Governor-General represent?

   _____

   _____

3. Who recommends the person for the position of Governor-General?

   _____

   _____

4. Who appoints the person selected to the position of Governor-General?

   _____

   _____

5. How long does the Governor-General hold this position?

   _____

   _____

6. Using the internet, search for the site of the Governor-General. Who was the first Canadian appointed to the position of Governor-General. In what year was he appointed?

   _____

   _____

7. What is the Governor-General's most important role?

   _____

   _____

8. Name three other responsibilities the Governor-General performs.

   _____

   _____

   _____

 # Exploring Canada

Name: _____

The Prime Minister

The _____ of Canada is called a prime minister. The prime minister is also the leader of the _____ _____ in the _____ of _____. The prime minister is _____ by the people of Canada. He/She usually governs for _____ years and then an _____ must be called by the Governor General.

The prime minister is the most _____ person in the government. In the House of Commons he/she _____ for the _____ country. The prime minister visits other countries to improve _____ and foreign _____. In the House of Commons he leads the other members in _____ and _____ on how to improve Canada and the Canadian way of living.

The prime minister chooses other members in his party help him _____ Canada. They are called his _____. this group of ministers is called a _____. The Cabinet discusses important _____ and _____ and _____ on them. The prime minister has the _____ say on all policies and he/she has the _____ to change any decision made by Cabinet.

The prime minister lives at an official residence at _____ in _____. Our present prime minister is _____ _____.

 # Exploring Canada

Name: _____

The Cabinet

The Cabinet is a group of elected members chosen by the _____
_____ from the majority party in the House of Commons. The members of the
Cabinet are called _____. A minister is the _____ of a government
_____. Quite often the minister is given a department he know very
_____ about so a _____ _____ helps him to run it.

Each province must be represented by _____ minister. _____
provinces will have more than one minister. The Cabinet ministers and the prime minister
must work together as a _____. They make _____ decisions that will
affect the entire country. They decide which _____ will be passed and
whether the country will be at _____ or at _____. They also decide
how the country's _____ will be _____. The prime minister and the
Cabinet can _____ and _____ our taxes as well.

The Cabinet ministers must _____ on and _____ all policies made
by the Cabinet. If a Cabinet minister _____ support the policy he may
_____ or be _____ to resign by the prime minister.

prime minister	little	team
leader	one	raise
department	large	laws
deputy minister	important	lower
money	asked	war
peace	ministers	agree
defend	cannot	resign
spent		

 # Exploring Canada

Name: _____

Canada's Parliament

Parliament is the national _____ of Canada. It is made up of the _____, the _____ and the _____. The Senate is often referred to as the _____ _____ and the House of Commons is called the _____ _____.

The Senate

The Senate is a group of _____ and _____ appointed by the _____ _____ on the advice of the prime minister.

A Senator must be at least _____ years old and own property worth _____ and he/she must _____ in the province or territory for which he/she was appointed. A Senator must retire at the age of _____.

Senators carefully examine each _____ passed by the House of Commons. The Senate can _____ or _____ any bill it examines. The Senate also _____ and writes _____ on problems dealing with poverty, unemployment, old age, use of land, and Native affairs.

government	bill	Lower House
Governor-General	Crown	30
$4 000.00	reject	investigates
House of Commons	reports	Senate
live	men	women
Upper House	pass	75

 # Exploring Canada

Name: _____

The House of Commons

Complete each sentence with the correct information.

1. Members of the House are elected _____
   _____

2. The House of Commons seats _____

3. A member of Parliament can serve _____

4. Each session of Parliament begins with _____
   _____

5. Parliament sits for _____

6. The sittings of Parliament begin in September and end in _____

7. Parliament has recesses so _____
   _____

8. Each sitting in Parliament is organized and each day it has _____

9. On the agenda will be:
   _____
   _____
   _____
   _____

10. The best part of each day's sitting is _____

11. Members of the House enjoy Question Period because _____
    _____
    _____

12. The Speaker of the House makes sure _____
    _____
    _____

The House of Commons

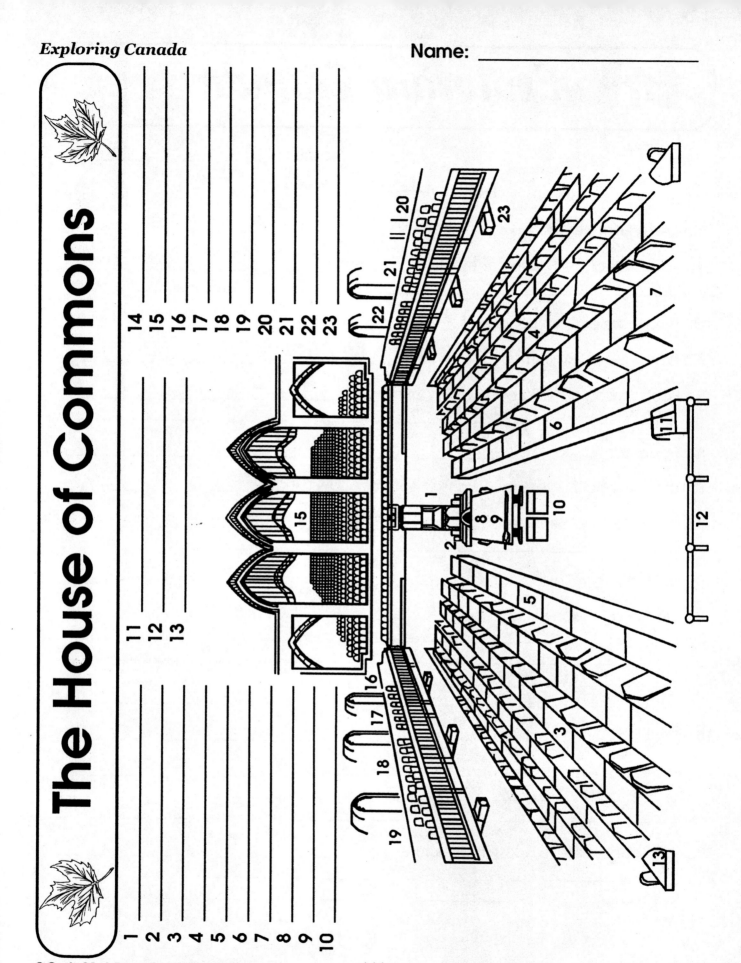

1
2
3
4
5
6
7
8
9
10

11
12
13

14
15
16
17
18
19
20
21
22
23

 # *Exploring Canada*

Name: _____

Sir John A.'s Confederation Quiz - True or False

1. A federal state is one united country. _____

2. In 1866, Canada was made up of four main provinces. _____

3. Today, Canada East is Ontario and Canada West is Québec. _____

4. Before Confederation Canada East and Canada West always got along well. _____

5. The Fathers of Confederation wanted the provinces to be united because they feared the Americans would invade them. _____

6. Confederation was an easy task as the communities were well informed and every one agreed on how to solve the problems. _____

7. The Fathers of Confederation wanted to break away from all ties with the Monarchy and British Parliament. _____

8. The Fathers of Confederation wanted to name Canada "The Kingdom of Canada". _____

9. The British North America Act became Law on July 1, 1967. _____

10. Sir John A. Macdonald became Canada's first Prime Minister. _____

11. Canada's birthday is celebrated on July 1 with a big celebration in every community across Canada. _____

12. Canada's official title is "The Dominion of Canada". _____

13. Canada West wanted to be free of English domination. _____

14. The British North America Act did twelve things for the people and provinces. _____

15. The Americans did not like the name "Kingdom of Canada". _____

16. In order for Canada to grow and develop economically the provinces had to unite. _____

 # Exploring Canada

Name: _____

Canada's Government

1. Who is Canada's head of state?_____

2. Who is the Queen's representative in Canada? _____

3. What do you call the Queen's representative in the provinces and territories?
   _____

4. What is Canada's system of government called?_____

5. What are the three parts of parliament? _____
   _____

6. What are the three levels of government in Canada? _____
   _____

7. What do you call a law before it is passed? _____

8. How are members of Parliament chosen? _____

9. Who do members of Parliament represent? _____

10. How is the prime minister chosen? _____

11. When does an election have to be held according to the constitution? _____

12. What is the name of the premier of your province? _____

13. What is the name of the Lieutenant-Governor in yor province? _____

14. What is the name of the Prime Minister of Canada? _____

15. What is the name of the Governor-General of Canada? _____

 # Exploring Canada

Name: _____

Canada's Symbols

1. Which animal is an official symbol of Canada? Using the internet, search to find why this animal was chosen and when. Write your answer below.

_____
_____
_____
_____

2. What song is Canada's national anthem? When was it written and by whom? You will need to do some research to find this information. Both the library and the internet are good tools. Write your answer below, then write the words to our National Anthem.

_____
_____
_____
_____
_____
_____

3. What does Canada's flag look like? Draw and colour the flag. When did this flag become the flag of Canada? What flag was Canada's before that?

_____
_____
_____
_____

 # Exploring Canada

Name: _____

Provincial/Territorial Quiz

1. In which province or territory do you live? _____

2. Where is your province or territory located in Canada? _____
   _____

3. What is the capital city of your province or territory? _____

4. Who is the premier of your province or territory? _____

5. Which political party does your premier represent? _____

6. How many Cabinet ministers help your premier run the government? _____

7. What are the members of the Legislature called in your province or territory?
   _____

8. What is the short form for this title? _____

9. Who is your Lieutenant-Governor or Commissioner? _____

10. What is the name of the member of the Legislature who represents your riding or constituency? _____

11. What party does he/she represent? _____

12. Where is your representative's office located in your constituency? _____
    _____

13. What is the telephone number of his/her office? _____

14. How does your provincial or territorial government help the people? List the various services that is provides.
    _____
    _____
    _____
    _____
    _____

Exploring Canada

Canada's Capital Region

Ottawa, Canada's capital, is located on the border of the province of Ontario. It was made the capital of the Province of Canada in 1857 by Queen Victoria. Today, a much larger Capital Region serves as a frame for Canada's capital. The Capital Region consists of Ottawa and Gatineau as well as numerous small towns and rural communities. It covers an area of 4715 square kilometres that stretches out on both sides of the Ottawa River to include parts of two Canadian provinces: Québec to the north and Ontario to the south. The region has a population of 1 081 000 (2000). The Capital Region is one of Canada's most bilingual communities. Nearly half a million people speak both English and French fluently.

Ottawa is a city of national symbols. Its buildings, statues, museums and memorials represent the history and values of Canadians. Visitors take away a deeper understanding of Canada and its people. These symbols also highlight Canada's democracy, provinces and territories, Canadian land-scapes, Canadians in war and peace, Canadian heroes, Canadian achievers and Canada in the world.

Parliament Hill and the **Peace Tower** symbolize Canadian democracy making **Canada one of the freest and most peaceful societies in the world. The Centennial** Flame represents Canada's provinces and territories. It has burned since 1961 and represents Canadian unity. Provincial and territorial flags fly along the length of Confederation Boulevard and in the Garden of Provinces in their honour.

The **National War Memorial** and the **Tomb of the Unknown Soldier** honour Canadians who died in war. Millions of tulips bloom in May in the Capital Region to remind us of the role Canada played helping The Netherlands during World War Two.

Modern and historic heroes are remembered in the Capital as well. Terry Fox, a modern day hero, ran halfway across Canada to raise money for cancer research in 1981. Today, a statue of him running can be seen on Wellington Street. Samuel de Champlain, a hero from the past, was a French explorer who travelled the Ottawa River in 1613 and founded a nation. His statue stands on Nepean Point honouring his efforts and achievements. Statues and monuments can be seen on and around Parliament Hill. They have been erected to honour Prime Ministers, Royalty and Fathers of Confederation.

There are more museums in Ottawa than in any other Canadian city. The Canadian Museum of Civilization celebrates the achievements of cultures from the present and the past. Other museums depict the history of Canadian farming, nature, money, air travel, science, technology, art, communication and photography. Canada's Capital Region is a wonderful place to experience Canadian history, visit national museums, view historic sites and monuments, and to become acquainted with the government and how it works.

 # Exploring Canada

Name: _____

Let's Research Canada's Capital Region!

Using your favourite internet search engine, run a search using the key words "Canada's Capital and Its Region".

At the site, locate information needed to complete the following activities. Record your answers on the lines provided.

1. How many statues are located on Parliament Hill?
    _____

2. List the names of the famous Canadians who have been honoured.
    _____
    _____
    _____
    _____

3. Choose one of the statues and find out why the person was recognized for his/her achievements.
    _____
    _____
    _____
    _____

4. How many monuments can you see in the city of Ottawa?
    _____

5. List the names of the monuments and their locations on the following chart.

Monument	Location

 # Exploring Canada

Name: _____

Ottawa's History Challenge

Ottawa's history has been an eventful one. Over the years, it has changed its face many times and is now the treasure house of Canada's heritage and a meeting place for all Canadians.

Carefully read the following events that took place in Ottawa's history.

Number the events in the order in which they happened:

____ In 1806, Wright built a raft out of squared timber and floated it down the Ottawa River to Québec City. This proved that logging in the Ottawa Valley was possible.

____ In the early 1850s, sawmills buzzed noisily, the air was filled with saw dust, lumber was piled high and great fortunes were made from the lumbering industry.

____ The Parliament Buildings of Canada were completed in 1866, just in time for Confederation which took place in 1867.

____ The first inhabitants of the Ottawa River Valley were the Algonquin Native People.

____ Although the north side of the Ottawa River (Wrights Town) hummed with activity in the 1810s and 1820s, the south side of the river was a virtual wilderness.

____ Since then, the Centre Block has been rebuilt and Ottawa has been transformed into a scenic, green capital city.

____ Etienne Brulé was the first European to explore the Ottawa River.

____ In time, the Ottawa Valley was the major timber-producing area in Upper and Lower Canada.

____ In 1613, Champlain, a French explorer, arrived in what is now the capital and made detailed maps of the Ottawa Region.

____ In 1826, Lieutenant-Colonel John By changed the south side of the Ottawa River when he and his workers began the construction of the Rideau Canal.

____ In 1857, Queen Victoria chose Ottawa to be the capital city of the United Province of Canada.

____ When the Rideau Canal was finished in 1832, many of the workers stayed on in the community called Bytown.

____ In 1916, the Centre Block on Parliament Hill was destroyed by fire. All that was left standing was the Library of Parliament.

____ In 1855, the name of Bytown no longer suited the growing town and it was incorporated as the City of Ottawa.

____ In 1899, Prime Minister Wilfrid Laurier said that Ottawa was not a handsome city so he created the Ottawa Improvement Commission to beautify the parks and to clean up the Ottawa River.

____ Barracks Hill was chosen as the site, and construction of the Parliament Buildings began in 1860.

____ The Great Fire of 1900 began in Hull and destroyed lumber mills and nearly two thousand buildings on both sides of the Ottawa River. This changed the face of Canada's capital.

____ In 1800, Philemon Wright and a group of colonists from Massachusetts settled on the north side of the Ottawa River below Chaudière Falls.

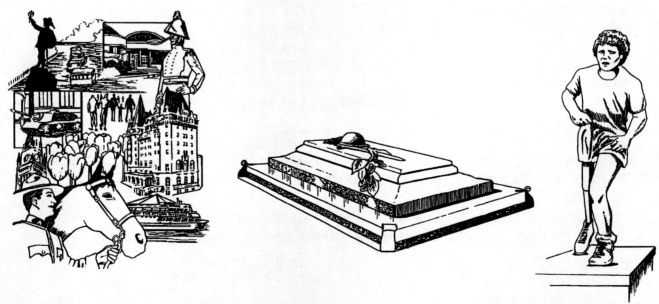

Exploring Canada

The Parliament Buildings

Canada's **Parliament Buildings** are a distinctive symbol recognized by Canadians and people around the world. Although these buildings come alive with the drama of modern day debates and discussions on a daily basis, the echoes of times and personalities of long ago still linger in the halls and chambers.

The Parliament Buildings stand stately on **Parliament Hill.** The **Centre Block** with its distinctive **Peace Tower** and library is flanked by the **East and West Block.** High vaulted ceilings, marble floors and dramatic lighting create an atmosphere of solemnity inside each building. Their walls bear lively details and decorations.

House of Commons

The House of Commons is found at the west end of the **Centre Block.** The **Chamber** is decorated in the traditional green of the British House of Commons. The rectangular chamber is constructed of Canadian white oak and Tyndall limestone from Manitoba. The ceiling is covered with Irish linen that was delicately painted after it was installed. The stained glass windows depict the floral emblems of Canada's provinces and territories and add bold, vibrant colour to this dignified room. A series of sculptures located below the windows explain the parts of Canada's Constitution.

The **Senate Chamber** is located at the east end of the Centre Block. This regal chamber is carpeted and upholstered in red with a ceiling of gold leaf. Hanging from the ceiling are two large bronze chandeliers. The upper walls are covered with murals depicting stirring scenes from World War I. The lower walls bear a frieze showing Canada's plants and animals carved in the Canadian white oak panelling.

The Senate Foyer

The House of Commons and the Senate are separated by **Confederation Hall** and the **Hall of Honour**. Gracefully arched ceilings and detailed sculpture decorate the halls. The **Library of Parliament** is located at the end of the Hall of Honour and is a showpiece of neo-gothic architecture. The parquet flooring is made from the wood of oak, cherry and walnut trees. The walls are panelled with Canadian white pine into which have been carved hundreds of flowers, masks, and mythical creatures. In the centre of the circular, domed room sits an impressive, white marble statue of Queen Victoria. The employees in this library use computer technology to provide information, reference and research services to members of parliament and their staff.

Library of Parliament

The Peace Tower

Rising above the Parliament Buildings is the well recognized Peace Tower. It was built to celebrate the end of World War One. The tower contains an observation area, a carillon of 53 bells and a Memorial Chamber.

The Centre Block also contains many important offices and facilities. The office of the Prime Minister and other party leaders are found in this building.

The East Block houses the restored offices of Canada's first Prime Minister, Sir John A. Macdonald, as well as offices for current parliamentary staff.

The West Block contains committee rooms and offices of members of the House of Commons and is not open to the public.

Exploring Canada

Name: _____

The Parliament Buildings

1. Neatly label the following diagram:

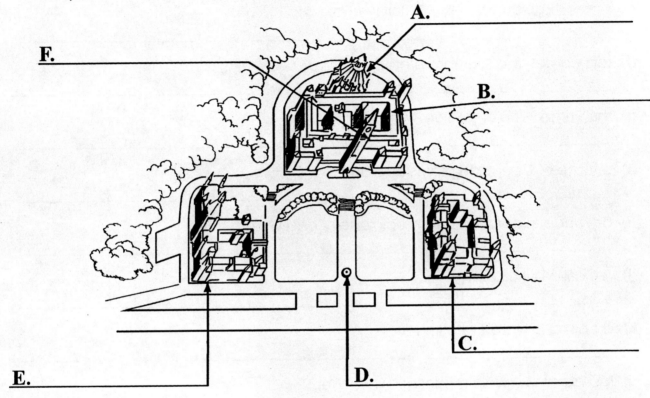

2. The Parliament Buildings are considered a highly recognized symbol of Canada. On the lines provided, record a list of other symbols that represent Canada.

   _____
   _____
   _____

3. Carefully read each group of words. On the line provided, record the location of each item in the Parliament Buildings.

   a) Peace Tower

   _____

   b) Sir John A. Macdonald's office

   _____

c) committee rooms and offices

_____

d) Parliamentary Library

_____

e) stained glass windows with floral emblems

_____

f) red carpet and red upholstered furniture

_____

g) the Prime Minister's office

_____

h) a frieze of Canadian plants and animals

_____

i) a wooden floor made from oak, cherry and walnut trees

_____

j) a Carillon of 53 bells

_____

k) a ceiling covered with Irish linen

_____

l) murals on the walls depicting World War I

_____

m) a large white marble statue of Queen Victoria

_____

4. Using your favourite internet search engine, run a search using the key words "Parliament Buildings of Canada". Read the information to find out more facts and record three new facts on the lines provided.

_____

_____

_____

_____

_____

_____

National Monuments of Canada

Research a Monument

Using your favourite internet search engine, run a search using the key words "Canadian Memorial Monuments".

Click on the web site called 'We Will Remember War Monuments in Canada'.

Locate the name of your province or territory. Click on your province's or territory's name.

Click on the name of a monument.

View the monument's picture and read the information.

You may wish to view other monuments as well.

Choose the monument that was the most attractive and had an interesting description.

Write a brief report about it in on the worksheet provided.

Illustrate the monument.

Make sure your report answers all the journalistic questions:

Who?   What?   Why?   When?   Where?   How?

RECONCILIATION
PEACE KEEPING MON

The Reconciliation, Peacekeeping Monument

Exploring Canada

Name: _____

_____

(Name of Monument)

Exploring Canada

Name: _____

Canada's National Heritage Sites

Parks Canada is responsible for Canada's program of commemorating historical sites, people, and events. The most common form of commemoration is by a plaque or a simple marker. There are many historical sites located throughout Canada.

Using your favourite internet search engine search for "National Heritage Sites of Canada".

Click on a site that you wish to investigate.

Find out the following information:

1. What is the name of the heritage site that you visited?

   _____

2. Where is the heritage site located?

   _____

   _____

3. What special events take place at the site?

   _____

   _____

   _____

   _____

   _____

4. Why is this heritage site important?

   _____

   _____

   _____

   _____

5. When is the heritage site open?

   _____

6. How much does it cost to visit it?

   _____

Exploring Canada

Name: _____

National Landmarks of Canada

Using the internet or an encyclopedia, find the location of the following landmarks.

National Landmark	Location
1. Hawthorne Cottage	
2. Red Bay	
3. Queenston Heights	
4. Bar U Ranch	
5. Alexander Graham Bell	
6. Fisgard Lighthouse	
7. Grand Pré	
8. Province House	
9. York Factory	
10. S.S. Klondike	
11. Ryan Premises	
12. Sainte-Anne-de-Bellevue Canal	
13. St. Andrews Blockhouse	
14. Saint-Louis Mission	

Exploring Canada

L'Anse aux Meadows

A Newfoundland & Labrador Landmark

Nearly 1 000 years ago **Leif Eiriksson**, a Viking explorer, and a crew of 30 men anchored in an inviting bay somewhere along the coast of North America 300 years before Christopher Columbus discovered America. When the men stepped ashore, they discovered a low and rolling landscape covered with lush meadows and thick forests. A small stream flowed from a nearby lake. Spectacular tides amazed them and when the tide went out, the entire bay became dry land.

The Viking explorers were delighted with what they saw. They decided to set up camp on the shore. Short trips into the country made them realize how rich this country was. An abundance of salmon lived in the many streams. There was plenty of timber located in the thick forests and the climate was so mild the grass stayed green all year. One day, a crew member wandered from the settlement and discovered grapes growing wild in the forest. After this exciting discovery, Leif Eiriksson called the new land "Vinland", Land of Wine.

Eiriksson and his men returned to Greenland the next summer. Their ship was heavily loaded with a cargo of timber and grapes in the form of wine or raisins. The people in Greenland were happy to see the timber since they had no timber suitable for building.

The news of Eiriksson's successful trip aroused the interest of other Greenlanders. Thorfinn Karlsefni, an Icelandic trader decided to make an expedition to Vinland. His expedition may have had 135 men, and fifteen women, livestock, and three or more ships. The same camp established by Eiriksson was used and the Vikings spent several summers exploring the land and collecting lumber, pelts and other things that could be sold in Greenland or Europe.

Eventually the Vikings met the Native people who lived on the land. They were called "Skraelings" by the Vikings. In time, the Skraelings and the Vikings clashed. The Vikings returned to Greenland as they were greatly outnumbered by the natives and feared for their lives.

On one of the voyages by either Leif Eiriksson or Thorfinn Karlsefni, the explorers settled for a time **at the head of Newfoundland's Great Northern Peninsula at a place called L'Anse aux Meadows.**

In this area, they built a small community on a narrow gravel terrace close to a water-logged peat bog and a small stream. No one knows how long they stayed but they lived there long enough to build houses, workshops and a small forge. At this forge, iron was smelted for the first time in the New World. The buildings decayed and nature reclaimed the land after they left.

In 1960, a Norwegian explorer and writer **Helge Ingstad**, came upon the site at L'Anse aux Meadows. It took Helge and his wife, archaeologist Anne Stine Ingstad, and an international team of archaeologists from Norway, Iceland, Sweden and the United States eight years to excavate the site. They found the lower parts of the walls of eight Viking buildings from the 11th century. The walls and roof had been made of sod laid over a framework of wood. These buildings were the same as the ones used in Iceland and Greenland just before and after the year 1000. In the middle of the floor of each building was a long, narrow fireplace used for heating, lighting and cooking.

Near the site today, sod houses have been recreated and the artifacts discovered are on display. In 1977, L'Anse aux Meadows was decleared a National Historic Site and is cared for by Parks Canada. In 1978, the site was declared a United Nations World Heritage Site.

 # Exploring Canada

L'Anse aux Meadows

A Newfoundland & Labrador Landmark

L'Anse aux Meadows

L'Anse aux Meadows is a favourite tourist attraction in Newfoundland and Labrador.

Use the words in the box to complete the story about L'Anse aux Meadows.

Print the words on the lines provided.

Many years ago, Leif Eiriksson, a _____, and his men _____ and _____ in parts of North America. They camped somewhere along the _____ of North America 300 years before Christopher _____ discovered America. Eiriksson and his men found this new land to be rich in _____, _____ and wild _____.

Other Vikings heard of Eiriksson's successful _____ and _____ to this new land. Some Vikings built a _____ on Newfoundland's Great Northern peninsula at a place called L'Anse aux _____. Here they built houses and workshops from wood and _____. A _____ was built to smelt _____ for the first time in North America. In time, the Vikings returned to _____ and the buildings _____ and the place became _____ with plants.

Helge Ingstad, his wife and a group of archaeologists excavated the _____ at L'Anse aux Meadows for _____ years. They discovered the _____ parts of the _____ of eight buildings and other artifacts at the site.

Near the site today stands a _____ Viking Community. There are sod and timber _____ and artifacts on display. In 1977, L'Anse aux Meadows was declared a National _____ Site. In 1978, it became a United Nations _____ Site.

Viking	Columbus	salmon	Meadows	Heritage	lived	coast
re-created	timber	community	houses	trip	lower	Historic
grapes	travelled	explored	walls	rotted	Greenland	
forge	overgrown	eight	sod	iron	site	

Exploring Canada

Fundy Bay and the Hopewell Rocks

A New Brunswick Landmark

The **Bay of Fundy** is located between the provinces of New Brunswick and Nova Scotia. The Bay is 290 kilometres long. The mouth of the Bay is 100 kilometres wide and it is between 120 and 215 metres deep. This funnel-shaped bay gradually narrows until it splits to form Chignecto Bay and the Minas Basin. Chignecto Bay becomes gradually shallower and splits into Shepody Bay and Cumberland Basin. The Shepody Bay narrows and splits again into the Memramcook and Petitcodiac Rivers.

At the junction of the Memramcook and Petitcodiac Rivers, the **Hopewell Rocks** are found. Shepody Bay, at this point, is 2.5 kilometres wide and at low tide is about fourteen metres deep.

The Hopewell Rocks at Cape Hopewell, New Brunswick are one of the most popular tourist attractions in the province. This site is also the location of the highest tides in the world. For thousands of years, glaciers, fractures, and the incessant action of the Fundy Tides have hollowed out caves and pillars in the rocky cliffs to form the peculiar "flower pot rocks" (Hopewell Rocks). During low tide, the rocks and the beach around them may be explored. At high tide, the rocks form small islands. These fascinating natural sculptures provide homes for many animals who live in the grasses and trees that grow on the rocks.

During July for a six week period, two to three million shorebirds congregate in waves along several key locations in the upper reaches of Fundy Bay. It is their only stop on a 5 000 kilometre southbound journey from summer breeding grounds in the Arctic to their winter home along the southeast coast of South America, in the Guianas and Brazil. These birds are drawn to the Hopewell Rocks, Johnson's Mills and Mary's Point along the Bay of Fundy shoreline in New Brunswick because of a small amphipod, the mud shrimp, which lives in the salty mud. The mud shrimp burrows into the mud, then as the tide recedes, scurries to the surface to find mating burrows. On the mud flats there may be 10 000 to 20 000 tiny crustaceans in a square metre.

Flocks of shorebirds such as species of sandpipers and plovers may be seen feasting on these tasty treats. A single bird can eat 10 000 to 20 000 mud shrimp during a single tidal cycle. Each flock of birds stays in the area only long enough to double their weight to gain energy reserves for the remainder of their non-stop 4 000 kilometre flight over the ocean to South America.

During the shorebird migration, roosting areas such as the Hopewell Rocks are protected and visitors are requested to keep their distance to allow the birds to complete their mission undisturbed.

Exploring Canada

Fundy Bay and the Hopewell Rocks

A New Brunswick Landmark

Many years ago, native Mikmaq knew the shores of the Bay of Fundy better than anyone. They told many colourful legends to explain the tides and the rock formations.

Read each Mikmaq legend carefully.

Choose **one** of the legends.

Illustrate the legend on a large sheet of paper.

Hopewell Rocks

Mikmaq Legends - The Tide

One day Glooscap, the great native god, decided to take a bath. Glooscap told Beaver to build a dam across the mouth of the bay to keep the high water in so he could bathe himself. Beaver did as he was told and built a dam.

Whale became angry. he wanted to know why the water had stopped flowing. Glooscap did not want to anger Whale so he told Beaver to go and break the dam. Whale did not want to wait that long. He began to break the dam apart with his great tail.

This caused the water to slosh back and forth with such force that it still does it today.

The Hopewell Rocks - Legend One

Many years ago, there were some poor Mikmaq who were slaves to angry whales who lived in the Bay. One day, some of the slaves decided to run away from the whales. They ran as far as the beach, but were then captured by the whales. The slaves were turned to stone. Their images today are encased in the stones called the Hopewell Rocks.

Legend Two

In the waters of the Bay lived a terrible monster. Everyone was afraid of it. The monster loved to eat white porpoises and to catch Mikmaq natives to make them its slaves.

One day, the monster was very hungry. He ordered his slaves to go fishing for the white porpoise. As soon as the slaves were out of the monster's sight, they began to run away. When the monster discovered the slaves were gone, he swung his tail up and down angrily. His tail churned up the water near the cliffs and carved the strange shapes we see in them today.

 # Exploring Canada

Queen Charlotte Islands

A British Columbia Landmark

The **Queen Charlotte Islands** are located in the Pacific Ocean off the coast of British Columbia. There are 1 884 islands in the archipelago (a group of islands). Seven of the largest islands are - from north to south-Langara, Graham, Moresby, Louise, Lyell, Burnaby and Kunghit Island. The two main islands are Graham Island and Moresby Island which are separated by the very narrow Skidgate Channel. The population of the Islands is approximately 6 000 inhabitants.

The Islands in the archipelago are covered with a mixture of snow-topped mountains, misty forests and windswept sandy beaches. Their coastlines are cut with deep fiords that plunge into the sea. The total land area of the Queen Charlotte Islands is approximately 9 984 square kilometres and stretches 250 kilometres from north to south.

The Queen Charlotte Islands are also called "Haida Gwaii", islands of the people, and have been home to the Haida people for at least 7 000 years. At one time, approximately 14 000 people lived in 126 known village sites. Europeans discovered the islands and brought the disease smallpox to the Haida people. Many of the people died from the disease. The Haida left their villages and moved to Skidgate. Many of these abandoned villages contain the best remaining examples of original native totem poles in the world. The Haida village called "Ninstints" has been declared as a World Heritage Site in recognition of the history of mankind.

The Queen Charlotte Islands are often called the "Canadian Galopagos" due to their evolutionary showcase. Theories suggest that parts of the Islands escaped the last ice age, forming a glacial refuge for certain forms of plant and animal life. There are plant species and different sub-species of birds, fish and mammals found nowhere else in the world.

Millions of seabirds use the Islands as breeding colonies due to immense amounts of plankton during the spring and early summer. Some of the colourful species seen are tufted puffins, horned puffins, rhinoceros auklets, black-footed albatross, black oyster catchers and pigeon guillemots. Along the coast, bald eagles and their nests can be seen. The saw-whet owl is one of the unique island sub-species.

Blue, sperm, minke, sei, gray, finback, humpback and killer whales all frequent the waters around the Queen Charlotte Islands. They feed on the large areas of plankton in the waters.

Steller sea lions congregate at the southern tip of the Queen Charlotte Islands to mate and give birth to their pups. This is one of the largest breeding rookeries on the west coast of North America. Harbour Seals are frequently seen either swimming near shore or lying on beaches.

The Queen Charlotte Islands' black bear is the largest black bear in the world. Black-tailed deer and raccoons were species introduced to the Islands. Unfortunately, they are causing many ecological problems. They do not have natural predators and are increasing in numbers. The raccoons steal eggs and young from bird colonies and the deer are over-browsing the cedar trees.

The forests on the Islands are filled with giant stands of sitka spruce, western hemlock, red and yellow cedar. The floors of the forests are deeply carpeted with a hundred types of mosses, salal bushes, huckleberry and ferns.

This quiet wilderness of beautiful islands offers an escape to a roughly-edged paradise. There are countless beaches, streams, fishing holes, coves and abandoned Haida villages to explore. Visitors who come to visit these enchanting islands will never forget their visit.

Name: _____

Queen Charlotte Islands
A British Columbia Landmark

There are many things to see when you visit the **Queen Charlotte Islands**.

In the word search, **circle** the names of the sights you would see on the Islands.

In the totem pole, print the name of each one found. There are **20** sights to find.

```
K A J B I C H D B G E F F C G B H A I Z J Y K
N T O T E M P O L E S M E L D P U F F I N S X
O N P O Q O P R A Q S R T S U T V U W V X W Y
M Z L A K U B J C C I D H F E R N S G E F F E
P U O V N N W M K X L Y K O Z J A I B H C G D
T Q S R R T S Q B P T O U R N V M W L X K Y J
A E B D C A D C E F B G A E H Z M O S S E S I
Z F Y G X I W H A V I U J S T K S L R M Q E N
X G W H V N I U R J T K S T L R M Q N P O A P
F Y E Z D S C I S L A N D S B A A B Z C Y L X
H N I M J L K K L J M I N H O G P F Q E R S D
U W H A L E S S O T B A L D E A G L E S V P W
L J K K J L I M H N G O F P E Q D R C S B T A
I B E A C H E S M H N G R A C C O O N S O F P
B U A V Z W Y X X Y W Z V U A T B S C R D Q E
M H A I D A V I L L A G E S L O K S N J M I L
N P O Q P R Q S R T S U T E V U W P V X W Y X
Y H Z G A F B E C D D C E A F B G R H A D I Z
O C E D A R T R E E S I N L M J L U K K E L J
P V Q U R T S S T R U Q V I P W O C X N E Y M
G A L B A T R O S S F W E O D X C E B Y R A F
H H I G J F K E L D M C N N O B P T Q A R Z I
I C J B K A L Z M Y N X O S W P V R Q U R T O
D D E C F B G A H Z I Y J X K W L E V M U N R
T S A W W H E T O W L S E S F R G E Q H P I D
U J V K W L X M Y N Z O A P B Q C S R D S E S
```

Answer Key

Booklet A:

Page 1   big, United States, ten, three, Ottawa
Page 2   Answers may vary.
Page 3   beautiful, proud, red, white, maple leaf, eleven
Page 4   people, countries, languages, English, French
Page 5   maple leaf, emblem, flag, penny, maple trees, colour
Page 6   Canada Goose, black, white, bird, water, south, spring
Page 7   beaver, Canadian nickel, brown, flat, lodge, trees
Page 8   country, Canada, policeman, horse, jacket, black, brown

Brandon Beaver:

Page 32   Answers may vary.
Page 33   B Sounds: bee, bed, ball, beaver   M Sounds: mountains, moose, milk, mountie
Page 34   Match the Sound: beaver b; Canada c; goose g; mountains m; flag f
Page 40   Math: **1.** 4 pennies   **2.** 3 dimes   **3.** 6 nickels   **4.** 4 quarters   **5.** 3 toonies   **6.** 5 loonies

Booklet B:

Page 49   Canada, second, Canadians, 31 499 560 (estimated in 2003), English, French
Page 50   provinces, three, capital city, large, island, Nunavut, Northwest Territories
Page 51
1. Newfoundland & Labrador; St. John's
2. Prince Edward Island; Charlottetown
3. New Brunswick; Fredericton
4. Nova Scotia; Halifax
5. Québec; Québec City
6. Ontario; Toronto
7. Manitoba; Winnipeg
8. Saskatchewan; Regina
9. Alberta; Edmonton
10. British Columbia; Victoria

1. Nunavut; Iqaluit
2. Yukon; Whitehorse
3. Northwest Territories; Yellowknife

Page 52   red, white, symbol, maple leaf, eleven, white, red, coasts
Page 53   maple leaf, maple, lumber, maple syrup, hunted, trapped, forests, Canada Goose, south, spring, world, red, jackets, black, hats.
Page 54   Ottawa, Parliament Buildings, Royal Canadian Mounted Police, Prime Minister, Tulip Festival, Winterlude, Canal, Chateau Laurier, Hall
Page 55   mosaic, ship, countries, settled, parts, home, work
Page 56   **a)** 3 nickels   **b)** 1 nickel & 2 pennies   **c)** 3 dimes   **d)** 1 dime & 1 penny   **e)** 2 quarters   **f)** 2 dimes & 1 quarter   **g)** 1 dime & 1 quarter & 1 nickel   **h)** 3 nickels
Page 57   **a)** 9 cents   **b)** 9 cents   **c)** 10 cents   **d)** 6 cents   **e)** 15 cents   **f)** 13 cents   **g)** 15 cents   **h)** 14 cents   **i)** 17 cents
Page 58   **a)** 6 cents   **b)** 4 cents   **c)** 8 cents   **d)** 2 cents   **e)** 5 cents   **f)** 6 cents   **g)** 7 cents   **h)** 7 cents   **i)** 8 cents
Page 59   **1.** 5 cents   **2.** 13 cents   **3.** 14 cents   **4.** 10 cents   **5.** 4 cents   **6.** 15 cents
Page 60   **1.** winter   **2.** summer   **3.** fall   **4.** spring   **5.** fall   **6.** spring   **7.** winter   **8.** summer   **9.** summer   **10.** winter
Page 61   **Word Puzzle**

1. maple leaf
2. province
3. beaver
4. territory
5. Ottawa
6. hockey
7. flag
8. ten
9. country
10. mountains

Page 62   **1.** wol**f**   **2.** el**k**   **3.** ow**l**   **4.** bea**r**   **5.** raccoo**n**   **6.** walru**s**   **7.** fla**g**   **8.** oppossu**m**   **9.** islan**d**   **10.** rabbi**t**   **11.** fo**x**   **12.** dolla**r**

Page 63 Long o - mole   Short o - fox   Long e - leaf   Short e -red
Long i - island   Short i - river   Long a - maple   Short a - Canada
Long u - Yukon   Short u - skunk

Page 64 1. chop 2. chips 3. chirp 4. chime 5. chimney 6. child 7. chin
8. chick 9. chair 10. church

Booklet C:

Page 1 country, North America, village, second, United States, Atlantic Ocean, Pacific Ocean, Arctic Ocean

Page 2 provinces, territories, Inuit, Ottawa, Ontario, name current Prime Minister and party, O Canada, From Sea to Sea

Page 3 ten, three

1. Newfoundland & Labrador; St. John's
2. Prince Edward Island; Charlottetown
3. New Brunswick; Fredericton
4. Nova Scotia; Halifax
5. Québec; Québec City
6. Ontario; Toronto
7. Manitoba; Winnipeg
8. Saskatchewan; Regina
9. Alberta; Edmonton
10. British Columbia; Victoria

1. Nunavut; Iqaluit
2. Yukon; Whitehorse
3. Northwest Territories; Yellowknife

Page 4 provinces, territories, Québec, French, Montreal, Québec City, forestry, Ontario, one third, Ottawa, Toronto, automobiles

Page 5 Manitoba, Saskatchewan, Alberta, British Columbia, farms, wheat, cattle ranches, trees, lumber, east, Newfoundland & Labrador, Nova Scotia, New Brunswick, Prince Edward Island, smallest, fishing

Page 6 three, Yukon, Northwest Territories, Nunavut, newest, Inuit, Dene, cold, barren, mining, hunting, trapping

Page 7 Label map

Page 8 national, red, white, maple leaf, eleven, strength, purity, February 15, 1965, Union Jack

Page 9 capital, Ontario, Ottawa River, Parliament Buildings, government, Prime Minister, politicians, laws, Rideau Canal, skate, Winterlude, Tulip Festival

Page 72
1. p o l a r b e a r (long o, short e)
2. p o r c u p i n e (long o, short u, long i)
3. c h i p m u n k (short i, short u)
4. p r o v i n c e (short o, short i)
5. m a p l e s y r u p (long a, short u)
6. t o t e m p o l e (long o, short e, long o)
7. M a n i t o b a (short a, short i, long o, short a)
8. N u n a v u t (short u, short a, short u)
9. v i l l a g e (short i, short a)
10. W h i t e h o r s e (long i, long o)

Page 73
1. maple leaves 2. territories 3. provinces 4. cities
5. moose 6. communities 7. deer 8. Canada Geese
9. Arctic Foxes 10. countries 11. oceans 12. walruses

Page 74 **Cross Word Puzzle**

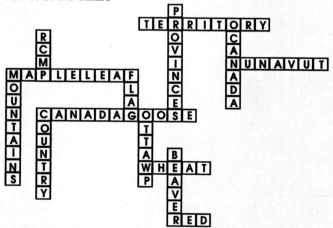

Page 80
1. 5 - thousands, 6 - hundreds, 3 - tens, 2 ones
2. 7 - hundreds, 3 - tens, 3 - ones
3. 2 - thousands, 0 - hundreds, 6 - tens, 3 - ones
4. 9 - thousands, 9 - hundreds, 9 - tens, 0 - ones
5. 6 - hundreds, 0 - tens, 7 - ones
6. 1 - thousand, 8 - hundreds, 5 - tens, 1 - one
7. 3 - thousands, 9 hundreds, 5 - tens, 4 - ones
8. 2 - hundreds, 7 - tens, 3 - ones

Page 81 A)
1. 5 000 + 0 + 90 + 5
2. 9 000 + 700 + 80 + 6
3. 600 + 50 + 3
4. 8 000 + 0 + 0 + 2
5. 7 000 + 500 + 0 + 4
6. 2 000 + 0 + 60 + 5
7. 1 000 + 100 + 10 + 1
8. 6 000 + 700 + 30 + 1
9. 900 + 50 + 6
10. 3 000 + 600 + 0 + 5

B) 1. 5 632 2. 761 3. 8 070 4. 7 214 5. 5 001 6. 5 000 7. 6 340 8. 890

Page 82 A) 1. 1 561 2. 2 073 3. 666 4. 9 999 5. 5 001 6. 3 063 7. 896 8. 7 953

B)
1. 4 564, 4 565, 4 566, 4 567
2. 2 020, 2 021, 2 022, 2 023
3. 3 460, 3 461, 3 462, 3 463
4. 683, 683, 684, 685
5. 1 002, 1 003, 1 004, 1 005
6. 6 782, 6 783, 6 784, 6 785

Page 83 A) 1. 541 2. 1 051 3. 873 4. 513 5. 6 102 6. 1 102 7. 4 906
8. 1 511 9. 3 200 10. 9 740

B)
1. 9 630, 9 632 2. 3 259, 3 261 3. 2 002, 2 004 4. 698, 700
5. 8 013, 8 015 6. 5 999, 6 001 7. 709, 711 8. 7 612, 7 614

Page 84 A)
1. five hundred, five
2. one thousand, six hundred, seventy-three
3. five thousand, six hundred, forty
4. two thousand, five hundred, thirty-one
5. three thousand, thirty
6. four thousand, eight hundred, seventy-one
7. six hundred, ninety-nine
8. nine thousand, three hundred, eighty

B) 1. > 2. < 3. > 4. > 5. < 6. < 7. <
8. > 9. > 10. <

Page 85
1. bear, pear
2. raccoon, spoon
3. beaver, cleaver
4. ox, socks
5. goat, boat
6. skunk, trunk
7. moose, goose
8. woodchuck, truck

Page 86
1. Alberta
2. Northwest Territories
3. Saskatchewan
4. British Columbia
5. Québec
6. Prince Edward Island
7. Ontario
8. Newfoundland & Labrador
9. Manitoba
10. Nova Scotia
11. New Brunswick
12. Yukon
13. Nunavut

An Introduction to Canada: *(page 93)*
1. Answers may vary.
2. Russia (17 075 200)
   Canada (9 976 140)
   United States (9 629 091)
   China (9 596 960)
   Brazil (8 511 965)
   Australia (7 686 850)
   India (3 287 590)
   Argentina (2 766 890)
   Kazakhstan (2 717 300)
   Sudan (2 505 810)
3. The size of Canada and its different climatic conditions and physical features would take a long time to explore.
4. Answer may vary.

The First Canadians: *(page 95)*
1. Map should show the route from Russia across the Bering Strait to Alaska to Canada.
2. The Inuit are the descendants of the first immigrants to Canada. Inuit means "the people". Inuit live inthe northern part of Canada, from Labrador to Hudson's Bay and north into the Arctic Circle
3. They followed the animals for food and clothing.
4. Answers may vary.
5. After the last Ice Age, the level of the ocean water caused the land bridge to disappear beneath it. This body of water is now called the Bering Strait.

Viking - Warriors and Explorers: *(page 97)*
1. The Vikings came from Denmark, Norway, and Sweden.
2. Answers may vary.
3. Route to be shown on a map.
4. The climate was good; the farmland was fertile.
5. Answers may vary.

Jacques Cartier and the Settlers from France: *(page 99)*
1. He was looking for a route to the Orient.
2. They might have been talking about the animals and plant life. Answer may vary.
3. France has lost interest in exploring the New World since Cartier did not find any riches.
4. Answers may vary.

Samuel de Champlain and the Settlers from France: (page 101)

1. Scurvy is a disease caused by the lack of vitamin C in the diet. It is characterized by swollen and bleeding gums, extreme weakness and bright spots on the skin. The eating of fresh vegetables and fruits helps to prevent it.
2. It would be easy to defend against enemies and would give them an easier route into the interior of New France.
3. He may have had difficulty with the Natives.
4. He was exploring the land looking for places where there were fur-bearing animals; mapping the territory.
5. Answers may vary.
6. They would use them as a guide while travelling.

The Colonizing of New France: (page 103)

1. Settlers would be useful in establishing different outposts for the fur traders.
2. A seigneury was a large section of land granted by the King of France.
3. The seigneur's duties were: to grant land to the censitaire; keep a record of the upkeep; help to pay for the cost of building a church; and build roads and bridges.
4. The censitaire's duties were: to pay the seigneur; work three or four days a year on the seigneur's land; build a house on the section of land that he was granted; cultivate the land and harvest the crops.
5. The winters were long and cold. The meat and vegetables ran out. The Natives often caused problems because the felt the colonists were taking over their land. The fur traders and the English settlers often caused problems.

The Fight Over Fur!: (page 105)

1. The people in Europe wanted fur for hats, gloves, and coats. The demand for fur steadily grew.
2. A pelt is the furry skin of a dead animal.
3. They would buy beaver, fox, raccoon, bear, wolf, etc.
4. It is 330 years old (2 000). Answers will change as the years pass.
5. The English had the same number of trading posts as the fur-traders of New France. The English began battling the French for their trading posts. The English captured Québec and won the war. Answer may vary.
6. The Loyalists were people who supported the British government while they were living in the United States during the American Revolution. The British were in power and they were loyal to the Monarchy. They felt safe under British Rule.

Changes in the New Colony: (page 107)

1. Québec   2. Ontario
3. They were having difficulties with Great Britain. In order to establish control in North America, the Americans decided to attack Canada.

4. A peace negotiator would try to make both sides happy by agreeing to certain things.
5. There are no guards or army defending the border. People can cross freely into both countries.

Confederation Comes to Canada: (page 109)

1. They didn't like the way the British government was running its North American colony.
2. The colony needed new roads, more schools and a better form of local government to keep up to its rapid growth.
3. Ottawa was chosen because it was close to Lower Canada and this would keep the French happy. It was a safe distance away from the American border.
4. Canada Day is held on July 1.
5. Work had already begun on the construction of the Parliament Buildings.

The Young Nation Grows: (page 111)

1. Manitoba joined in 1870 and British Columbia in 1871.
2. They were not interested in the union. They were successful farmers and fishermen and their shipbuilding industry was thriving. Prince Edward Island's colony was self-sufficient and the Islanders were quite satisfied with things as they were.
3. There was a need for an efficient way of shipping goods from eastern Canada to the west coast.
4. George Stephen, Donald A. Smith, William Cornelius Van Horne, Sir John A. Macdonald, workers from countries all over the world, e.g. China, Poland, Ukraine, Germany, British Isles.
5. People could communicate more quickly.
6. The lines could be repaired more quickly because the workers could travel by train to the problem area.

Problems in Western Canada: (page 113)

1. The North West Mounted Police wore scarlet tunics (jackets), grey riding breeches, black riding boots, and spurs. Their hats were either white cork helmets or caps shaped like pillboxes. Blue breeches with a yellow stripe replaced the grey breeches.
2. The Métis were mixed-blood people. They were neither white nor native. White men who came to North America often married Native women. The children of these marriages were known as Métis.
3. They felt that the new nation was destroying their hunting grounds and trespassing on their property. Answers may vary.
4. Answers may vary.

Into the Twentieth Century: (page 115)

1. According to 2003 Statistics:
Canada - 32 207 113
Japan - 127 214 499
United States - 290 342 554
Great Britain - 60 094 648
Russia - 144 526 287

China - 1 286 975 468
Canada has the lowest population.
2. timber, gold, steel, etc.
3. The trade unions helped the people make more money and improved working conditions.
4. Women fought for the right. They wanted equality.
5. "Cultural mosaic" means that Canada's population is a blending of many different cultures.
6. Canada was very large and needed people to farm the land and to work in the factories. These new settlers helped Canada to become a stronger country industrially and to grow bigger in population.

Canada and the World: *(page 117)*
1. Macdonald encouraged immigrants to come to Canada. He set up ways of protecting Canadian products from cheaper American-made goods. Laurier helped to build Canada's own navy.
2. Answers may vary.
3. Answers may vary.
4. Expo '67 - Montréal
Olympic Games - summer 1976 - Montréal
Olympic Games - winter 1988 - Calgary
5. Answer may vary.
6. February 15, 1965

Where is Canada?: *(page 119)*
second; northern; North America; United States; Mexico; 9 976 140; Russia
A continent is one of the seven dry land masses on the earth.
An ocean is a great body of salt water - oceans cover three quarters of the earth's surface.
Africa; Asia; Antarctica; Australia; Europe; North America; South America
Arctic Ocean; Atlantic Ocean; Pacific Ocean; Indian Ocean

Canada's Borders: *(page 120)*
Map: 1. Arctic Ocean   2. Alaska
      3. Pacific Ocean   4. Hudson Bay
      5. Atlantic Ocean   6. The United States
1. A border is the side or edge or boundary of anything. It can be a line which separates one country, state or province from another. It can be a coastline.
2. Pacific Ocean; Alaska
3. Atlantic Ocean
4. Arctic Ocean; Hudson Bay
5. United States
6. 13   7. No   8. 11   9. 2

Canada's Provinces and Territories: *(page 121)*
1. ten; territories
2. Alberta; British Columbia; Manitoba; New Brunswick; Newfoundland & Labrador; Northwest Territories; Nova Scotia; Nunavut; Ontario; Prince Edward Island; Québec; Saskatchewan; Yukon Territory

3. Prince Edward Island
4. Nova Scotia, Newfoundland & Labrador, New Brunswick, Prince Edward Island
5. Manitoba, Saskatchewan, Alberta
6. Yukon Territory, Northwest Territories, Nunavut
7. A) **Map - Canada's Provinces & Territories:**
   1. Newfoundland & Labrador
   2. Prince Edward Island
   3. Nova Scotia   4. New Brunswick
   5. Québec   6. Ontario
   7. Manitoba   8. Saskatchewan
   9. Alberta   10. British Columbia
   11. Yukon Territory   12. Northwest Territories
   13. Nunavut

   B) **Map - Canada's Capital Cities:**
   1. St. John's   2. Charlottetown
   3. Halifax   4. Fredericton
   5. Toronto   6. Ottawa
   7. Québec   8. Winnipeg
   9. Regina   10. Edmonton
   11. Victoria   12. Whitehorse
   13. Yellowknife   14. Iqaluit

Let's Research Canada!: *(page 122)*
1. Nunavut   2. Québec
3. Prince Edward Island   4. Edmonton
5. Regina, Victoria   6. British Columbia, Alberta
7. Winnipeg   8. Toronto
9. Trillium   10. Northwest Territories
11. Ontario   12. Québec City
13. New Brunswick   14. Prince Edward Island
15. Nova Scotia   16. Newfoundland & Labrador
17. Charlottetown   18. Fredericton
19. Prince Edward Island   20. British Columbia

Physical Regions of Canada: *(page 123)*
Answers may vary.

Important Rivers of Canada: *(page 124)*
1. Ottawa River, St. Maurice River, Saguenay River
2. Albany River, Moose River, Rupert River, Eastmain River
3. Churchill River, Nelson River, Severn River, La Grande River
4. St. Lawrence River
5. Fraser River, Skeena River
6. North Saskatchewan River, South Saskatchewan River
7. Mackenzie River, Peel River, Coppermine River, Black River
8. Yukon River
9, 10, 11. Answer may vary.

How Long are the Rivers in Canada?: *(page 125)*
1. Mackenzie River - 4 241 km - Arctic Ocean
2. Yukon River - 3 185 km - Bering Sea
3. St. Lawrence River - 3 058 km - Atlantic Ocean
4. Columbia River - 2 000 km - Pacific Ocean
5. Peace River - 1 923 km - Lake Athabasca

6. Churchill River - 1 609 km - Hudson Bay
7. Fraser River - 1 370 km - Pacific Ocean
8. Ottawa River - 1 271 km - St. Lawrence River
9. Athabasca River - 1 231 km - Lake Athabasca
10. Laird River - 1 115 km - Mackenzie River

Rivers and Lakes of Canada: *(page 126)*

1. a) Québec   b) Ontario
   c) Ontario   d) Ontario
   e) Alberta, British Columbia
   f) British Columbia
   g) Manitoba, Saskatchewan
   h) Saskatchewan, Alberta
   i) Ontario   j) Québec
   k) Ontario, Québec   l) Ontario
   m) Alberta, Northwest Territories
   n) British Columbia   o) Ontario
   p) British Columbia   q) Saskatchewan
   r) British Columbia   s) New Brunswick
   t) Newfoundland &Labrador
2. a) Grand Lake, Smallwood Reservoir
   b) Lake St. John, Lake Abitibi, Lake Mistassini
   c) Lake Simcoe, Lake Ontario, Lake Nipissing,
      Lake Nipigon, Lake of the Woods,
      Lake St. Clair, Lake Huron, Lake Erie
   d) Lake Winnipeg, Lake of the Woods,
      Lake Winnipegosis, Reindeer Lake
   e) Lake Athabasca, Reindeer Lake
   f) Lake Louise, Lake Athabasca
   g) Kootenay Lake, Lake Okanagan
   h) Grand Lake
   i) Lake Gary
   j) Great Slave Lake, Great Bear Lake, Lake Aberdeen

The Population of Canada: *(page 128)*

1. second; ten million; 32 million; uninhabited;
   rugged; severe
2. Nunavut - 28 100
   Yukon Territory - 29 800
   Northwest Territories - 40 800
   Prince Edward Island - 138 500
   Newfoundland & Labrador - 533 700
   New Brunswick - 757 000
   Nova Scotia - 942 600
   Saskatchewan - 1 015 700
   Manitoba - 1 150 000
   Alberta - 3 064 200
   British Columbia - 4 095 900
   Québec - 7 410 500
   Ontario - 11 874 400

Natural Vegetation Regions: *(page 129)*

1. coniferous, deciduous
2. low shrubs, mosses, lichens
3. British Columbia
4. Alberta, Saskatchewan, Manitoba
5. Northwest Territories, Nunavut, Ontario, Québec,
   Newfoundland & Labrador
6. Newfoundland & Labrador, Nova Scotia,

New Brunswick, Québec, Ontario, Saskatchewan
7. Yukon Territory, British Columbia, Alberta
8. A coniferous tree bears needles and its seeds are in a
   cone. It does not lose its needles every year; spruce,
   pine, hemlock.
9. A deciduous tree bears leaves and then loses them in
   the autumn of every year; maple, elm, beech.
10. It is a large treeless area found above the treeline.

What is a Government?: *(page 139)*

government; exercise power; make; enforce; conduct
1. group; rules; whole; good; discourage; forbid
2. supreme power; authority; democractic; people;
   chief
3. accepted; right; power; loyalty; flag; national
   anthem
4. power; rules; laws
5. rules; laws; enforce; order

What is Canada's Government?: *(page 140)*

Paragraph 1: three; legislative; executive; judicial;
         laws; effect; broken; punish
Paragraph 2: democracy; monarchy; parliamentary;
         cabinet; federal
Paragraph 3: elect; govern; representative
Paragraph 4: monarchy, Queen Elizabeth II;
         Governor General
Paragraph 5: parliamentary; British Parliament
Paragraph 6: Cabinet; House of commons; people;
         responsible
Paragraph 7: federal; national; provincial; territorial;
         federation; power; laws

The Governor-General: *(page 141)*

1. The Governor-General is an appointed official.
2. The Governor-General represents Queen Elizabeth II.
3. The Prime Minister recommends the person for the
   position.
4. The Queen appoints the person selected to the
   position of Governor-General.
5. The Governor-General holds this position for five
   years.
6. Vincent Massey was appointed to the position of
   Governor-General in 1952.
7. The Governor-General opens every session of
   Parliament and reads the Speech from the Throne.
8. The Governor-General entertains foreign visitors.
   He/She honours Canadians who have performed
   good things for Canada. He/She opens important
   buildings.
9. Right Honourable Adrienne Clarkson is presently
   the Governor-General of Canada.

The Prime Minister: *(page 142)*

Paragraph 1: leader; majority party; House;
         Commons; elected; five; election
Paragraph 2: powerful; speaks; entire; trade; policies;
         debates; discussions

Paragraph 3:	govern; Ministers; Cabinet; issues; policies; votes; final; right
Paragraph 4:	24 Sussex Drive; Ottawa; answer will pertain to the present Prime Minister

The Cabinet: *(page 143)*

Paragraph 1:	Prime Minister; Ministers; leader; department; little; Deputy Minister
Paragraph 2:	one; Large; team; important; laws; war; peace; money; spent; raise; lower
Paragraph 3:	agree; defend; cannot; resign; asked

Canada's Parliament: *(page 144)*

government; Crown; Senate; House of Commons; Upper House; Lower House

The Senate: *(page 144)*

Paragraph 1:	men; women; Governor-General
Paragraph 2:	30; $4 000.00; live; 75
Paragraph 3:	bill; pass; reject; investigates; reports

The House of Commons: *(page 145)*

1. by the people during an election.
2. 302 members.
3. for five years.
4. the Speech from the Throne.
5. 27 weeks of the year.
6. June.
7. the members of Parliament can work in their regions or ridings.
8. an agenda.
9. routine business; committee reports; recording documents; Ministers' statements; presentation of petitions; introduction of bills (laws); debating legislation (laws)
10. the Question period.
11. they can ask the Ministers all kinds of questions about their departments and policies.
12. the Members of the House follow parliamentary rules and behave themselves in the House.

The House of Commons (Diagram): *(page 146)*

1. Speaker
2. Pages
3. Government Members
4. Opposition Members
5. Prime Minister
6. Leader of the Opposition
7. Leader of the second largest party in opposition
8. Clerk and Table Officers
9. Mace
10. Hansard Reporters
11. Sergeant-at-Arms
12. The Bar
13. Interpreters
14. Press Gallery
15. Public Gallery
16. Official Gallery
17. Leader of the Opposition's Gallery
18. MPs' Gallery
19. MPs' Gallery
20. MPs' Gallery
21. Speaker's Gallery
22. Senate Gallery
23. T.V. Camera

Sir John A. Macdonald's Confederation Quiz: *(page 147)*

1. True	2. False	3. False	4. False
5. True	6. False	7. False	8. True
9. True	10. True	11. True	12. True
13. False	14. True	15. False	16. True

Canada's Government: *(page 148)*

1. Queen Elizabeth II
2. Governor-General
3. Lieutenant Governor/Commissioner
4. Parliamentary
5. The Queen, the House of Commons, the Senate
6. Local, Provincial, Federal
7. a bill
8. elected by the people
9. the people of Canada
10. has the most elected Members of Parliament
11. every four years
12. Answers may vary.
13. Answers may vary.
14. Answers may vary.

Canada's Symbols: *(page 149)*

1. The beaver attained official status as an emblem of Canada when Royal assent was given on March 24, 1975.
2. "O'Canada" originally written by Calixa Lavallée (music), lyrics by Judge Routhier, performed in 1880; proclaimed Canada's national anthem in 1980.
3. February 15, 1965; prior to that date, Canada flew the Union Jack.

Provincial/Territorial Quiz: *(page 150)*

Answer will vary.

Let's Research Canada's Capital Region!: *(page 152)*

1. There are thirteen statues.
2. Sir John A. Macdonald; William Lyon Mackenzie King; Sir George-Étienne Cartier; Queen Victoria; Lester B. Pearson; John G. Diefenbaker; Alexander Mackenzie; George Brown; Thomas D'Arcy McGee; Robert Baldwin/ Sir Louis-Hippoyte Lafontaine; Queen Elizabeth II; Sir Wilfred Laurier; Sir Robert Borden
3. Answer may vary.
4. There are ten monuments.
5. a) The Canadian Tribute to Human Rights - Corner of Elgin and Lisgar Streets
   b) The Terry Fox Statue - 90 Wellington Street
   c) National War Memorial - Confederation Square
   d) The Peacekeeping Monument - Sussex Drive, corner of St. Patrick Street

e) Anishinabe Scout - was located below Champlain Monument

f) The Commonwealth Air Force Memorial - Gree Island, across from Ottawa City Hall

g) Never Again War Monument to Peace and Remembrance - near St. Joseph Boulevard and Alexandré - Taché Boulevard in Hull

h) The Colonel By Monument - Major's Hill Park, Ottawa

i) Champlain Monument - Nepean Point, Ottawa

j) The Tomb of the Unknown Soldier - in front of the National War Memorial

Ottawa's History Challenge: *(page 153)*

5, 10, 14, 1, 7, 18, 2, 6, 3, 8, 12, 9, 17, 11, 15, 13, 16, 4

The Parliament Buildings: *(page 157)*

1. A. Parliamentary Library
   B. Centre Block
   C. East Block
   D. Centennial Flame
   E. West Block
   F. Peace Tower

2. Answers may vary. Possible Answers: Canadian flag, maple leaf, Canadian Coat of Arms, maple tree, maple syrup, beaver, Canadian money, Bluenose Schooner, CN Tower, Bonhomme, moose, polar bear, totem pole, Royal Canadian Mounted Police

3. a) Centre Block   b) East Block
   c) West Block   d) Centre Block
   e) House of Commons   f) The Senate Chamber
   g) Centre Clock   h) The Senate Chamber
   i) Parliamentary Library j) Peace Tower
   k) House of Commons   l) The Senate Chamber
   m) Parliamentary Library

4. Answer may vary.

National Landmarks of Canada : *(page 162)*

1. Brigus, Newfoundland
2. Newfoundland
3. Niagara-on-the-Lake, Ontario
4. near Longview in Alberta
5. Baddeck, Nova Scotia
6. near Victoria, British Columbia
7. near Wolfville, Nova Scotia
8. Charlottetown, Prince Edward Island
9. Churchill, Manitoba
10. Whitehorse, Yukon
11. Bonavista, Newfoundland
12. West Montréal, Québec
13. St. Andrews, New Brunswick
14. Honey Harbour, Ontario

L'Anse aux Meadows: *(page 164)*

Paragraph One: Viking, explored, lived, coast, Columbus, salmon, timber, grapes

Paragraph Two: trip, travelled, community, Meadows, sod, forge, iron, Greenland, rotted, overgrown

Paragraph Three: site, eight, lower, walls

Paragraph Four: re-created, houses, Historic, Heritage

Fundy Bay and the Hopewell Rocks: *(page 166)*

Each illustration may vary.

Queen Charlotte Islands: *(page 168)*

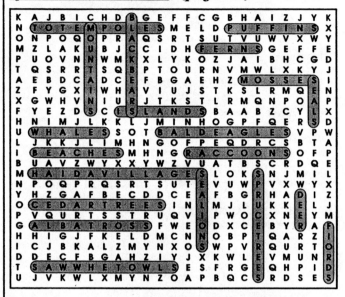

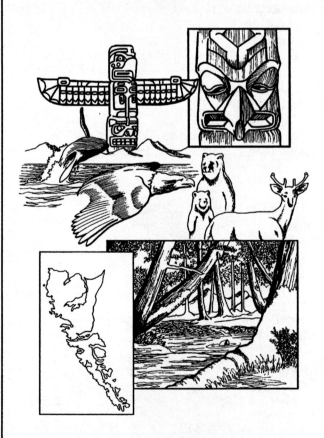